# Fibonacci For The Active Trader

# Fibonacci For The Active Trader

Derrik S. Hobbs

TRADINGMARKETS™
PUBLISHING GROUP

ISBN 0-9721229-7-4

Printed in the United States of America

Disclaimer

It should not be assumed that the methods, techniques, or indicators presented in this book will be profitable or that they will not result in losses. Past results are not necessarily indicative of future results. Examples in this book are for educational purposes only. The author, publishing firm, and any affiliates assume no responsibility for your trading results. This is not a solicitation of any order to buy or sell.

The NFA requires us to state that "HYPOTHETICAL OR SIMULATED PERFORMANCE RESULTS HAVE CERTAIN INHERENT LIMITATIONS. UNLIKE AN ACTUAL PERFORMANCE RECORD, SIMULATED RESULTS DO NOT REPRESENT ACTUAL TRADING. ALSO, SINCE THE TRADES HAVE NOT ACTUALLY BEEN EXECUTED, THE RESULTS MAY HAVE UNDER- OR OVERCOMPENSATED FOR THE IMPACT, IF ANY, OF CERTAIN MARKET FACTORS, SUCH AS LACK OF LIQUIDITY. SIMULATED TRADING PROGRAMS IN GENERAL ARE ALSO SUBJECT TO THE FACT THAT THEY ARE DESIGNED WITH THE BENEFIT OF HINDSIGHT. NO REPRESENTATION IS BEING MADE THAT ANY ACCOUNT WILL OR IS LIKELY TO ACHIEVE PROFITS OR LOSSES SIMILAR TO THOSE SHOWN."

*To Jessica for being an incredibly supportive wife who has sacrificed more than I will probably ever know to allow me to accomplish a life goal in writing this book.*

*To Sydney and Avery, Daddy's little girls. For the smiles and giggles that give me energy and perspective on life.*

# CONTENTS

# FOREWORD

If you had told me in the mid 90s that one day I'd be writing a foreword for a book on Fibonacci numbers, I would have thought you'd gone mad. You see, being a common-sense oriented trend trader, I've always seen these numbers as "hocus pocus." However, since then, I've seen former Head of Fidelity's trading desk Kevin Haggerty reference them in his column on TradingMarkets.com. Further, my business partner Kenneth Brown of Harvest Capital Management, who has been managing money for over 30 years, would *occasionally* mention Fibonacci levels.

Based on references from these credible sources, I thought it might be a good idea for me to learn more about the subject. After studying several books, I found myself very disappointed. All confirmed what I had originally feared. The books were vague, very esoteric and claimed that the numbers were magical. Further, none showed practical applications.

My feeling towards Fibonacci numbers all changed when I met Derrik Hobbs. He quickly admitted that they were not the "be-all-end-all" methodology. In our discussions, he mentioned triggers, protective stops, profit targets and alternative scenarios. In other words, how to *practically* apply the concepts in the real world.

Through working with Derrik, he showed me structure where I hadn't seen any before. To my amazement, his market calls were uncanny. Did they *always* work? Of course not, but that's where his practical approach made the methodology viable.

Do I think that Fibonacci numbers are magical? No. Do I think they can be used in trading and/or market analysis when applied in a practical way such as Derrik's? Yes.

Dave Landry
Author of *Dave Landry On Swing Trading*

# ACKNOWLEDGMENTS

**M**uch of the foundational material I will be sharing with you is a direct result of my interaction with Carolyn Boroden and through the educational materials of Robert Miner available at www.DynamicTraders.com.

I have simply expanded on what I have learned from these people and resources and will attempt to teach you, the reader, how I apply specific Fibonacci strategies in my own trading.

Larry Pesavento opened my eyes to the pattern recognition world and applying Fibonacci ratios to these patterns to create an edge in my trading. If you ever want to sit with someone who walks the talk, go spend a couple of days with Larry.

*With regard to actually putting this book together, there are a number of people I have to mention:*

Larry Connors: for providing the opportunity to put my thoughts on paper.

Eddie Kwong: for taking time to help me put this material in a presentable and readable format.

Dave Landry: for all the great suggestions and encouragement.

SYM Financial Corporation: for facilitating my wild ideas and creating an environment that allowed me to grow my skills as a trader.

Don DeYoung: for inspiring a son-in-law to tackle a project like this.

# Fibonacci For The Active Trader

# INTRODUCTION

When I first started trading 12 years ago, I was looking for the secret answer to trading. What was the one indicator, the one method, the one guru, that could tell me when to buy and sell?

To find it, I spent thousands of hours and dollars on books on the subject of technical analysis. I had myself tutored directly and indirectly by some extremely successful traders who have been in the thick of this business for years.

From my initial exposure to the market, to the present day, this 12-year journey has been filled with reward, humility, excitement, disappointment, and hard-knock education. Early on, my trading was very volatile and unpredictable. Much of that roller-coaster ride was due to the fact that I was making highly charged emotional trading decisions. I was floating from one trading system to another. I had no plan of attack.

Fortunately, it was this frustrating experience that became the driving force behind my desire to create a well-thought-out trading plan.

I am excited to say that what I have learned with Fibonacci analysis over the years has become my "holy grail." With this methodology, I have a plan of attack before each market day's open and can execute every trade with confidence. Sure I have losses and draw downs like every trader. **But I have the confidence that over a reasonable sample size, I will be profitable**.

So, when I was approached about writing a book on the trading strategies I use with Fibonacci, I was, naturally, excited. It is my honor to share with you the fruits of my labor. The information I'm about to share with you is extremely exciting to me.

**Not a trading day goes by that I am not applying Fibonacci analysis to the markets and, in turn, watching markets conform to my Fibonacci work.**

Now, let's take a peek at a few examples of Fibonacci at work and the potential decision-making power that Fibonacci puts in the hands of a trader. Don't get caught up in the specifics or math of these charts, for now. I'll take a couple of chapters later on to walk you through those details. For now, just observe some of the opportunities this analysis presents on a daily basis.

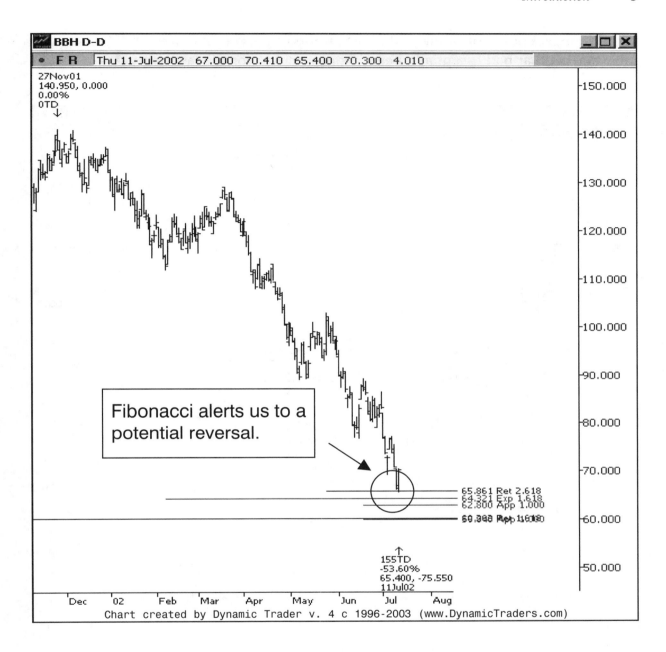

Fibonacci alerts us to a potential reversal.

By properly applying Fibonacci to price charts of stocks and commodities, we are able to project price zones where there is a high probability of a trend reversal occurring. To the trader, this represents tremendous profit opportunity. For example, the Biotechnology HOLDRs (BBH) was in a solid two-year down-trend and was trading down around $65. Fibonacci price support alerted us to one of these high-potential reversal zones between 60 and 65.

Over the next couple of months, the BBH traded up over 27 points or 42%. Not bad for a market that had essentially been trending down for the last two years.

As the next example will show, Fibonacci also alerts us to where price will likely reverse to the downside, creating opportunity to profit by selling short a stock, future, or commodity.

Below is a chart of Myriad Genetics (MYGN). Over the course of five weeks, this stock had rallied from a low of $16.00 per share to a high on August 15, 2002, of 26.20. That's a 64% upside move. At the $26 level, Fibonacci alerted us to the probability of a reversal to the downside. Not only were we looking for a reversal to the downside, but Fibonacci ratios had calculated a final price objective down around $13.22. I knew Fibonacci analysis was accurate, but this seemed like an aggressive target.

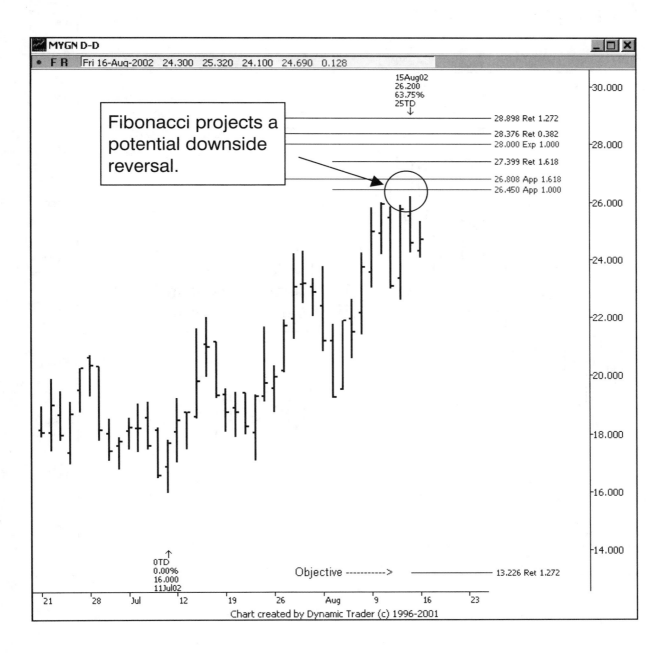

As you can see below, the accuracy of this analysis can be downright scary. Not only did MYGN reverse and go down when Fibonacci told us it would, but within a few short weeks it actually hit our profit objective. Who would have imagined that a stock that was up 63% trading at $26 would be trading at half of that value in just a few short weeks? I guess Fibonacci did!

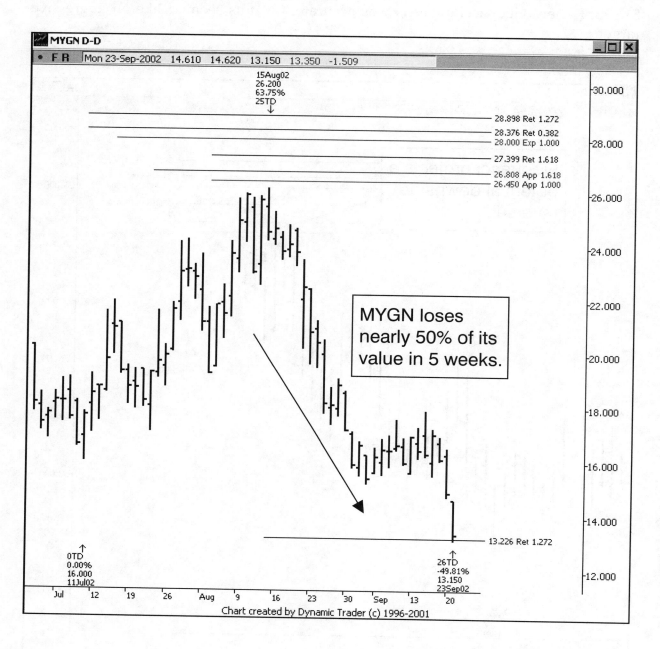

I've shown you a couple of examples on daily charts. It has been my experience and observation that the exact same analysis can be applied to almost any time frame as long as sufficient volume and data exists to create a measurable price bar. Below we are looking at a 60-minute chart of eBay (each bar represents 60 minutes of price activity). This stock has sold off over 4 points in four days. Most investors were heading for the exits. Fibonacci not only kept me in my seat but identified a key price support zone where there was a high probability that it would reverse.

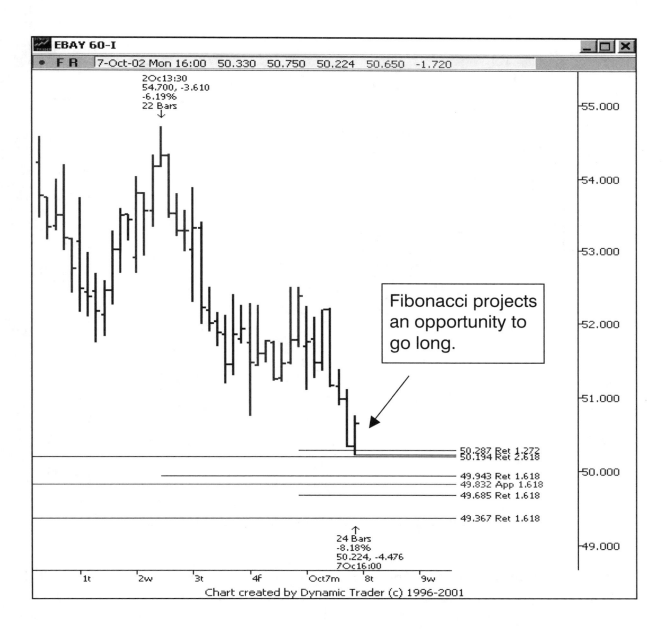

Fibonacci projects an opportunity to go long.

Chart created by Dynamic Trader (c) 1996-2001

The very next day, over six hours, eBay traded up over 3 points, or 6%. It would take at least three years at your local bank (at 2003 rates) to net those kind of returns in a savings account.

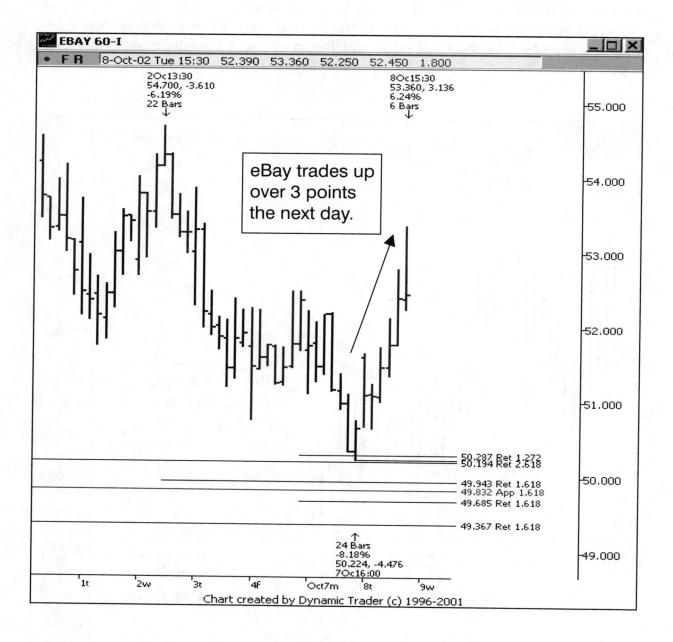

Trading opportunities like this one and the previous examples exist every day with Fibonacci. They exist on weekly, daily, and intraday charts. They occur in stocks, commodities, and futures contracts. And this analysis can be used and applied by daytraders, swing traders, and long-term traders alike.

I could go on with many more examples to show you how Fibonacci can help you identify trading opportunities in both stocks and futures and for different time frames. But instead, for the remainder of this book let me focus on teaching you how Fibonacci works and how you can apply it to your own trading.

Here is what you will learn as we work together chapter-by-chapter:

Chapter 1: Understanding How Fibonacci Works—In this chapter, I will explain what you need to understand about Fibonacci numbers in order to use them as a powerful tool in your trading.

## Section I: The Most Important Fibonacci Tools

Chapter 2: How To Find Important Support And Resistance Levels With Fibonacci— Next I will lay the foundation for the rest of the book by teaching you the basic step-by-step process that is common to all of the strategies that I will be teaching.

Chapter 3: Using FibZones To Identify High-Probability Reversals—You will then learn about FibZones. FibZones will provide you with a way of using multiple Fibonacci relationships to find reversals that have a higher-than-normal probability of occurring.

## Section II: My Favorite Fibonacci Strategies

Chapter 4: How To Enter Trends Using The Trend Trigger Strategy—Here, I will teach you one of my favorite Fibonacci trend-following strategies.

Chapter 5: The Reflection Reversal Method—Next, you will learn how repeating patterns in price can play a key role in helping you to identify the most powerful reversals.

Chapter 6: Trading Pullbacks Using The Triple Crown Strategy—This is my favorite pullback strategy. I will show you how, through the use of certain Fibonacci ratios and certain swing patterns, you can find excellent pullback trades at the beginning of a reversal or within a strong trend.

Chapter 7: Two-Step Patterns (TSP)—In this chapter I will teach you three variations on what I call "Two-Step Patterns." These three patterns will enable you to capture strong trends, enter the initial pullbacks of newly formed trends and trade major reversals in all time frames.

Chapter 8: Heisenberg 200—In this strategy, I will teach you how to determine when a violation of the widely watched 200-day moving average is likely a fake-out. I will teach you how to use Fibonacci in order to enter the powerful reversals that occur from these fake-out moves.

Chapter 9: Shark Attack—The next strategy I'll teach you is a special variation on double-top and double-bottom patterns. By using Fibonacci Extensions, you will be able to identify major reversals that occur off the second bottom (or top) of this pattern.

Chapter 10: Air Pockets—In this strategy, I will show you how to trade momentum moves that occur when a Fibonacci support or resistance zone is violated.

## Section III: It Boils Down To Proper Execution

Chapter 11: Entry Patterns: How To Enter The Trade—In this chapter, I will focus on teaching you the best patterns to use in order to trigger entries into trades. These entry patterns can then be applied to any of the strategies that I teach you in this book.

Chapter 12: Risk Management: Identifying And Managing The Key Areas Of Risk Control—Finally, I'll wrap up by teaching you the most important principles that enable you to achieve long-term trading success.

Now let's get started!

CHAPTER **1**

# UNDERSTANDING HOW FIBONACCI WORKS

In this chapter, I will teach you the basics of Fibonacci numbers and how they relate to the financial markets and trading. Also, I will show you the most important Fibonacci numbers to use in the strategies I'll be teaching you.

The Fibonacci numbers series and its unique properties was first written about by a mathematician named Leonardo de Pisa de Fibonacci (1170-1240).

The series starts like this:

$$1—1—2—3—5—8—13—21—34—55—89 \ldots$$

. . . and goes on from there.

Basically, the first two numbers are added to get the next number in the series. As you can see, this series goes on forever. What is fascinating about this number series is the ratio that is found when a number in the series is divided by the preceding number in the string (e.g., 8/5 or 55/34). This ratio, no matter where you go in the summation series, is right around 1.618.

Over the years, this ratio, 1.618, has been mentioned in writings, essays, and speeches by some of the greatest minds in science and mathematics. Why? Because it is found in the structure of a universal assortment of phenomena in the physical world. This includes nature, architecture, geometry, music, our DNA, and most relevant to us . . . *the financial markets.*

My theory is that Fibonacci ratios represent the purest forms of measurement of mass human behavior. It is a barometer for human hope, fear, and greed. For trading purposes, in scientific terms, Fibonacci is the mathematical structure of the growth and decay of psychological interest in a stock, futures contract, or commodity.

By understanding this structure, you can identify where the emotional shifts between euphoria and pessimism in the markets will come.

That, in turn, can be used by you to identify trading opportunities.

## THE KEY FIBONACCI RATIOS TO USE IN YOUR TRADING

In the next chapter, I will teach you how to use Fibonacci to find important support and resistance levels. I will show you how Fibonacci numbers are used in specific calculations to make these kinds of projections. What are the best Fibonacci numbers to use? Here they are.

The basic Fibonacci ratios I use are 1.618 and .618.

Besides these two numbers, other derivative ratios that I use in trading are:

**.382** = .618 squared. Also, the ratio between alternate numbers in the Fibonacci sequence is 2.618 or its inverse, 0.382

**.500** = divide the 2nd number by the 3rd in the Fibonacci sequence

**.786** = square root of .618

**1.000** = $1.618 \times .618$ (also used simply for symmetry measurements)

**1.272** = square root of 1.618

**2.618** = 1.618 squared

We will soon discuss the specific ways in which these ratios are used. The important point here is to know which ratios are used and how they are derived. At this point, you should have at least a basic understanding of the background of Fibonacci and the ratios we'll be using. If you are interested in furthering your education in the history of the Golden Mean or Fibonacci, all you need is a computer and Internet connection. There are thousands of articles and materials on the subject. Have fun!

# SECTION I

# THE MOST IMPORTANT FIBONACCI TOOLS

# CHAPTER 2

# HOW TO FIND IMPORTANT SUPPORT AND RESISTANCE LEVELS WITH FIBONACCI

When you have completed this chapter, you will be able to look at a chart, identify key highs and lows, and calculate Fibonacci price levels. You will also be able to identify a FibZone which is simply my term for a combination of at least three Fibonacci price levels within a relatively tight range. This concept will be the backbone of the rest of the book and *will enable you to perform the following Fibonacci price studies, the basic building blocks of all the strategies that I will be teaching you.*

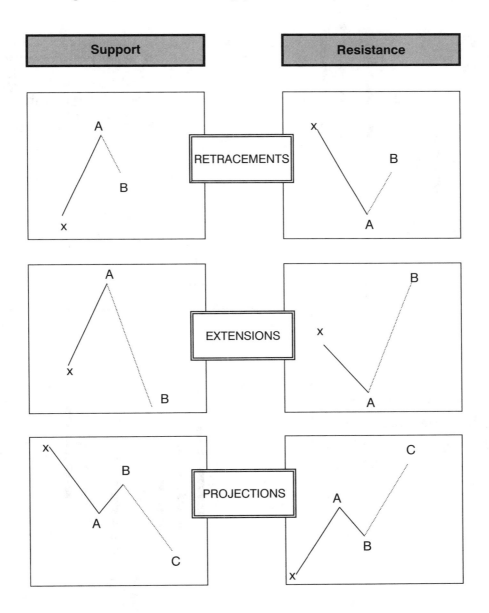

Before we can even think about calculating Fibonacci price support and resistance levels, we must learn to identify key swing points. Swing points are low or high points on a chart where price reverses direction. These are the key points used to calculate Fibonacci price levels. Rather than getting into a highly technical discussion of swing points, I am going to provide general guidelines to be followed in choosing these swing levels.

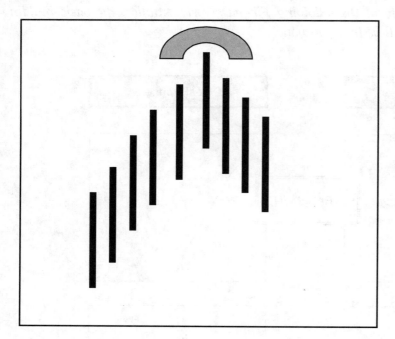

A swing high occurs when the current high has a lower high before and after it.

A swing low occurs when the current low has a higher low before and after it.

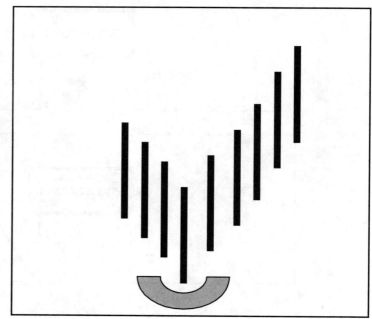

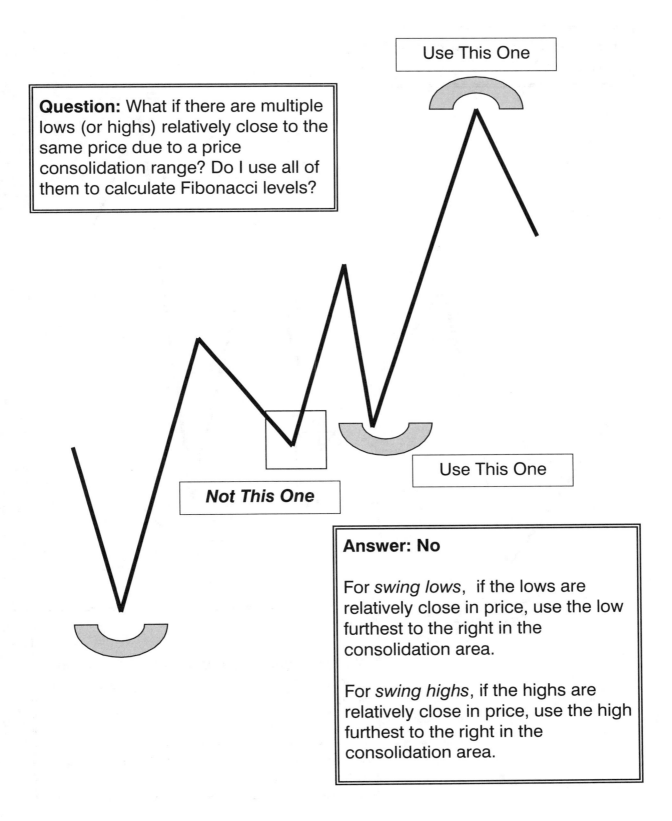

**Use This One**

**Question:** What if there are multiple lows (or highs) relatively close to the same price due to a price consolidation range? Do I use all of them to calculate Fibonacci levels?

**Not This One**

**Use This One**

**Answer: No**

For *swing lows*, if the lows are relatively close in price, use the low furthest to the right in the consolidation area.

For *swing highs*, if the highs are relatively close in price, use the high furthest to the right in the consolidation area.

**Question:** When is a swing point not valid to use?

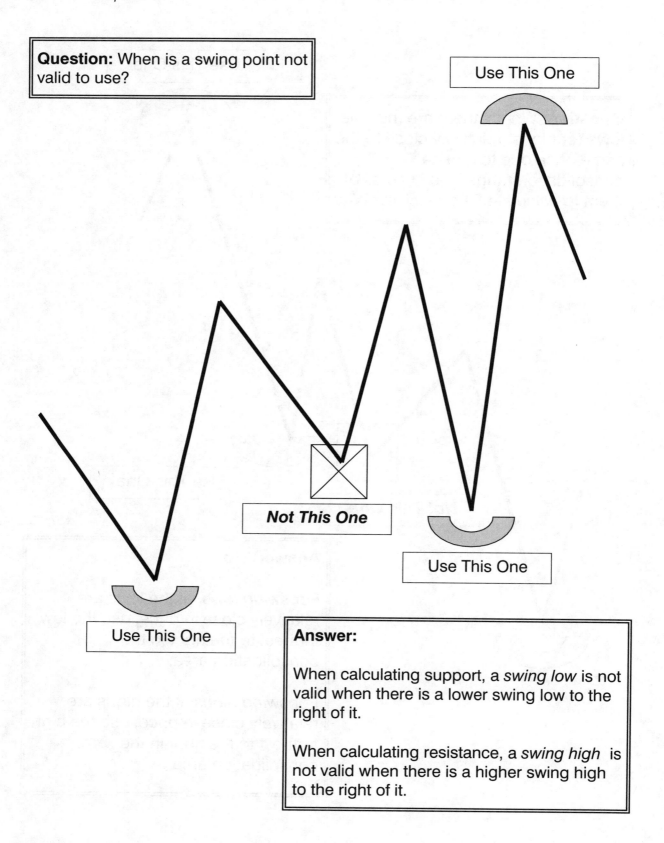

Use This One

Not This One

Use This One

Use This One

**Answer:**

When calculating support, a *swing low* is not valid when there is a lower swing low to the right of it.

When calculating resistance, a *swing high* is not valid when there is a higher swing high to the right of it.

# CREATING FIBONACCI LEVELS

Let's look at a few charts to get a feel for what to look for:

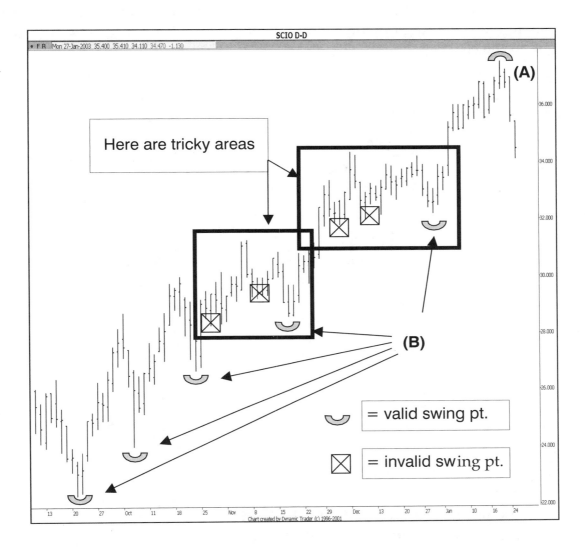

In the case of this chart, we are in an uptrend and the stock has just started to make a move to the downside (A) over the last three days. It will be my goal to calculate a price support zone with enough strength to stop the price action from going down and reverse it back up to continue the trend that has been in place. To do this I need to identify a swing high (A) and multiple swing low points (B). Please note that when we are calculating support levels *there is only one swing high and multiple swing lows.* This is the exact opposite for finding resistance in a downtrend (*one swing low and multiple swing high points*). It is the consolidation areas where swing points are most difficult to determine. Just apply our general rules discussed earlier.

Below is a stock in a downtrend. Once a swing low (A) is made in a downtrending stock, I look for swing high points (B) to use along with the current swing low (A). These are the swings to be used to calculate Fibonacci price resistance. In (1) and (2) below, you may ask why I wouldn't use both of those swing points. This was a situation where the swing high points were close in price, so I used the one furthest to the right on the chart.

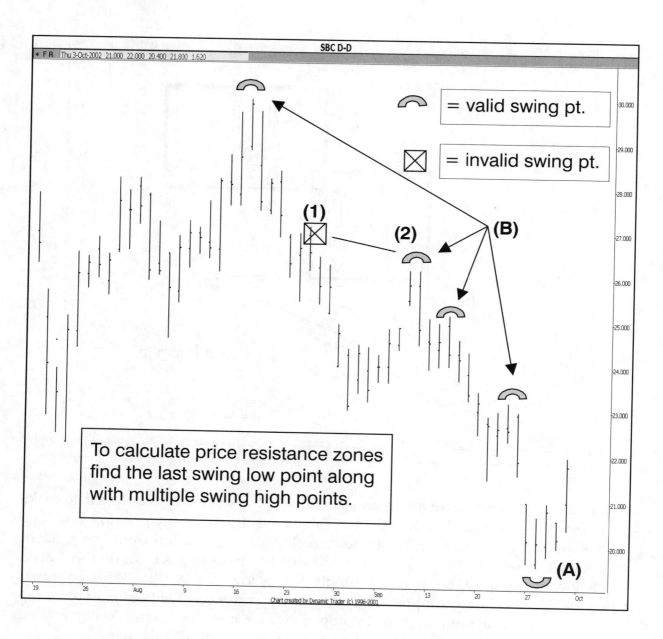

To calculate price resistance zones find the last swing low point along with multiple swing high points.

# STRATEGY Q&A

*Question:* How many swing points do you use to calculate your Fibonacci levels?

*Answer:* I'll go back as many as eight consecutive swing points. Beyond that it would be wise to shift to a higher time frame chart to analyze support and resistance. So, if you are studying a 30-minute chart and have gone back eight swing points, I suggest if you want to go back any further, shift to a daily chart.

*Question:* Are certain swing points more significant than others?

*Answer:* If a trend is in progress, I believe there are four swing points that carry the most weight. The first (A) is the swing point that was just made. Second (B) is the swing point made immediately before reversing into the trend that is in place. The third and fourth (C, D) are the last two swing points made in the direction of the trend before forming swing point A (see illustration).

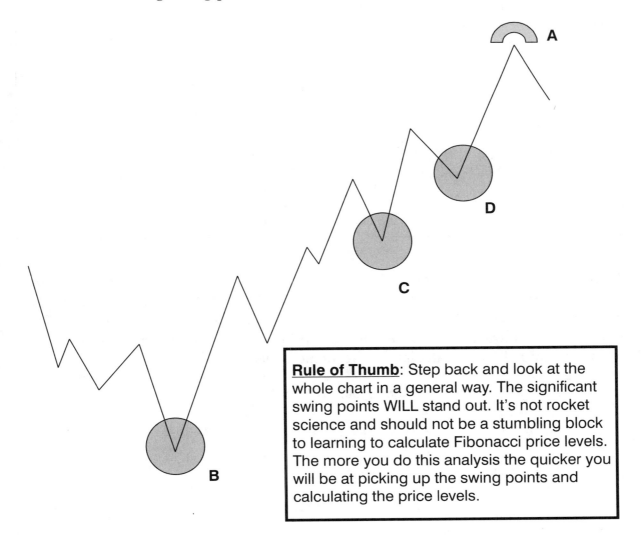

**Rule of Thumb**: Step back and look at the whole chart in a general way. The significant swing points WILL stand out. It's not rocket science and should not be a stumbling block to learning to calculate Fibonacci price levels. The more you do this analysis the quicker you will be at picking up the swing points and calculating the price levels.

# FIBONACCI PRICE STUDIES

Now that we have established how critical it is to the calculation of Fibonacci price levels to identify the key highs and lows on a chart, we can move on to the various types of Fibonacci price studies I use.

There are four types of Fibonacci price studies: retracements, extensions, projections, and expansions. Do not get hung up on the terminology as we will define each of these graphically to give you a solid visualization of what each means. Through the use of these four price studies, we will be calculating key areas of price support and resistance.

## Retracements

First let's take a look at a picture of a retracement:

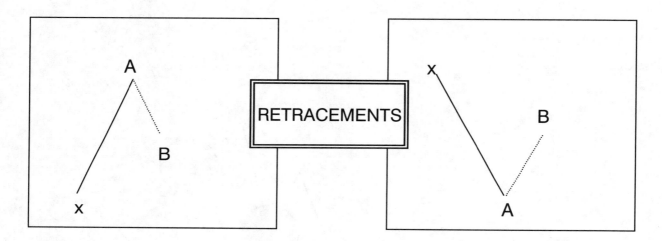

A retracement is simply a move in the opposite direction of the current trend. In a sense it is "recapturing" a portion of the move that was just made. In the illustrations above, the current trend is defined as X:A. When price reverses direction from A to B, it is "retracing" or recapturing a portion of the move from X to A. The Fibonacci ratios I use to calculate retracement levels are:

**.382 , .50, .618, and .786**

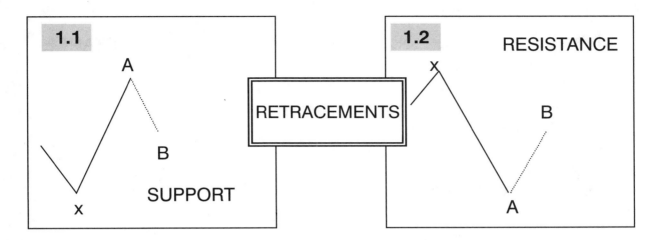

Retracements can be used to calculate support or resistance. When the move from X to A is up and price starts to go down (as in Figure 1.1), retracements are used to calculate support for B. Let's say X is $10 and A is $30.

First, let's calculate what the range of X to A is:

Price @ A: $30
Price @ X: $10

Range = $20.00

Next let's multiply this range by each Fibonacci ratio:

| Ratio | Points |
|-------|--------|
| 0.382 | $ 7.64 |
| 0.500 | $ 10.00 |
| 0.618 | $ 12.36 |
| 0.786 | $ 15.72 |

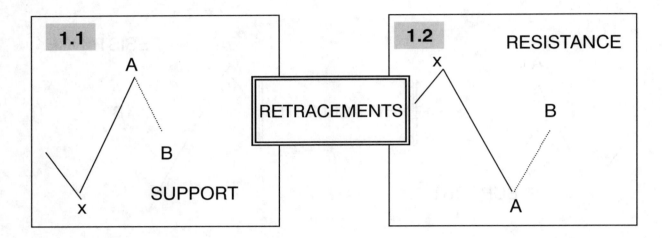

Finally, take the number (points) from each ratio and subtract it from A, which is $30.00. This will provide you with Fibonacci retracement levels:

| Ratio | Points | Pt. A | Fibonacci Retracement Levels |
|-------|--------|-------|------------------------------|
| 0.382 | $  7.64 | $ 30.00 | $ 22.36 |
| 0.500 | $ 10.00 | $ 30.00 | $ 20.00 |
| 0.618 | $ 12.36 | $ 30.00 | $ 17.64 |
| 0.786 | $ 15.72 | $ 30.00 | $ 14.28 |

So, if I were to ask you for the .618 retracement of swing X:A, the answer would be $17.64. The price levels in the table above represent Fibonacci price support decisions. The exact same analysis can be done for Figure 1.2 to calculate retracement levels acting as resistance. In Figure 1.2, X is 30 and A is 10. This time, instead of subtracting from A, we would add to A to determine price resistance levels:

| Ratio | Points | Pt. A | Fibonacci Retracement Levels |
|-------|--------|-------|------------------------------|
| 0.382 | $  7.64 | $ 10.00 | $ 17.64 |
| 0.500 | $ 10.00 | $ 10.00 | $ 20.00 |
| 0.618 | $ 12.36 | $ 10.00 | $ 22.36 |
| 0.786 | $ 15.72 | $ 10.00 | $ 25.72 |

Let's look at a couple of charts with retracements at work.

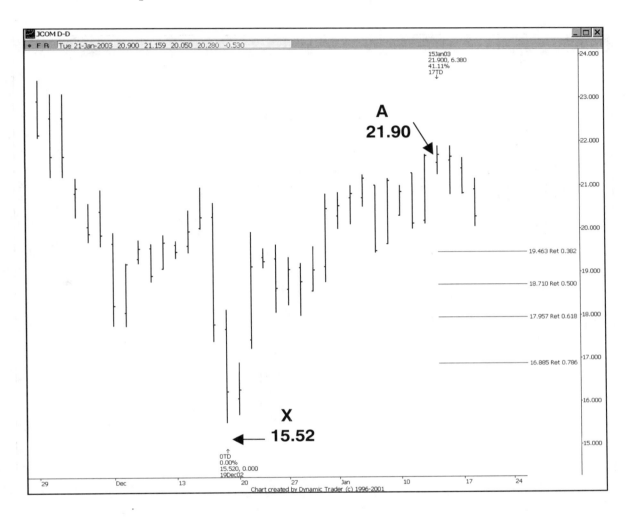

The daily chart of JCOM above put in a key low (X) at 15.52. Over the next 17 trading sessions JCOM traded up to (A) which was a high of 21.90. A reversal to the downside began. So, as soon as the key high (A) was established (with a lower high on each side), we could calculate the Fibonacci retracement levels that might act as support and stop the downside movement. Those levels are:

$$.382 = 19.46$$
$$.500 = 18.71$$
$$.618 = 17.95$$
$$.786 = 16.88$$

So, if I were to ask you what the .786 retracement of X:A is, you would answer 16.88.

Below is a chart in a downtrend that just put in a swing low (A).

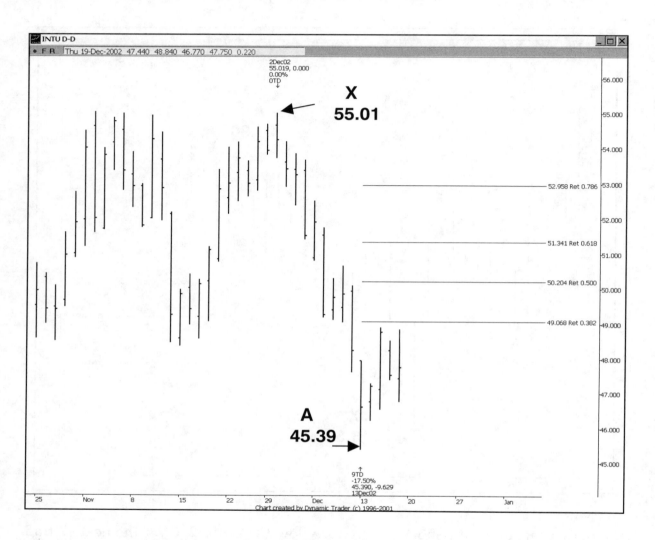

Any time a stock is in a downtrend and has just completed a significant low point (A), we can calculate Fibonacci retracement levels. Again, the goal is to determine how much the stock will "recapture" of the recent move down and where it has a likelihood to reverse and go back down. Based on the move from X to A, the Fibonacci retracement levels are:

$$.382 = 49.06$$
$$.500 = 50.20$$
$$.618 = 51.34$$
$$.786 = 52.95$$

# Extensions

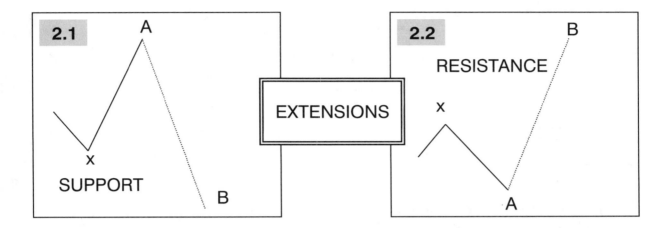

An **extension** is very similar to a retracement. It is "recapturing" a percentage of the previous move (X:A illustrated above). The difference between a retracement and an extension is that an extension recaptures more than 100% of the previous X:A move. Basically, B will go beyond X. The specific ratios I use for extensions are 1.272 and 1.618. Let's assume X is $20 and A is $30 in Figure 2.1. Below is the process to determine Fibonacci extension levels.

First, let's calculate what the range of X to A is:

Price @ A: $30
Price @ X: $20

Range = $10.00

Next let's multiply this range by each Fibonacci ratio:

| Ratio | Points |
|-------|--------|
| 1.272 | $ 12.72 |
| 1.618 | $ 16.18 |

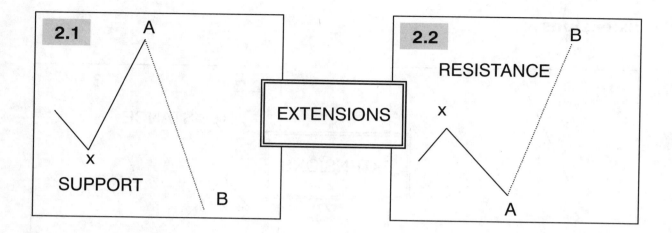

Finally, take the number from each ratio and subtract it from A, which is $30.00. This will provide you with Fibonacci extension levels:

| Ratio | Points | Pt. A | Fibonacci Extension Levels |
|-------|--------|-------|----------------------------|
| **1.272** | $ 12.72 | $ 30.00 | $ 17.28 |
| **1.618** | $ 16.18 | $ 30.00 | $ 13.82 |

So, if I were to ask what the 1.272 extension level of swing X:A in Figure 2.1 was, you would answer 17.28. This is a support level. Now we can do the same type of analysis to determine resistance. Let's look at Figure 2.2 where X is 30 and A is 20. Instead of subtracting from A (like in Figure 2.1), we will add to A to determine resistance:

| Ratio | Points | Pt. A | Fibonacci Extension Levels |
|-------|--------|-------|----------------------------|
| **1.272** | $ 12.72 | $ 20.00 | $ 32.72 |
| **1.618** | $ 16.18 | $ 20.00 | $ 36.18 |

Let's look at a couple of charts with extensions at work.

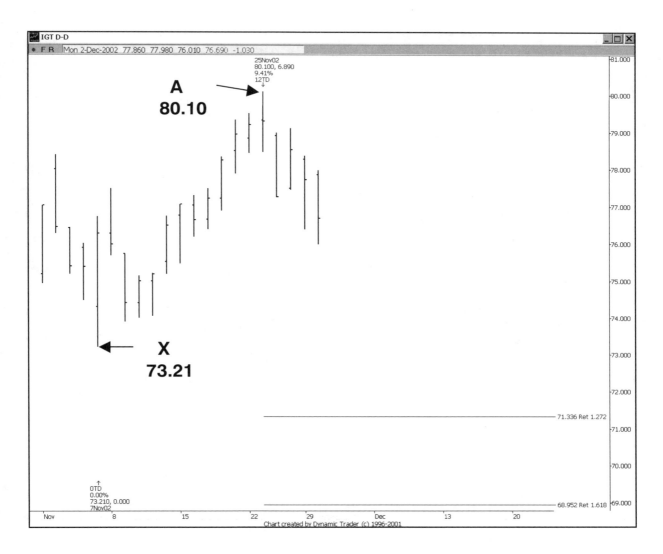

The daily chart of IGT above put in a swing low point (X) at 73.21. Over the next 12 trading sessions IGT traded up to (A), which was a high of 80.10. A reversal to the downside began. So, as soon as the swing high (A) was established, we could calculate the Fibonacci extension levels that might act as support and stop the downside movement. Remember, extensions are basically retracements of greater than 100% of the X to A move. The specific ratios we use are 1.272 and 1.618. Those levels came in at:

$$1.272 = 71.33$$
$$1.618 = 68.95$$

Check this out!

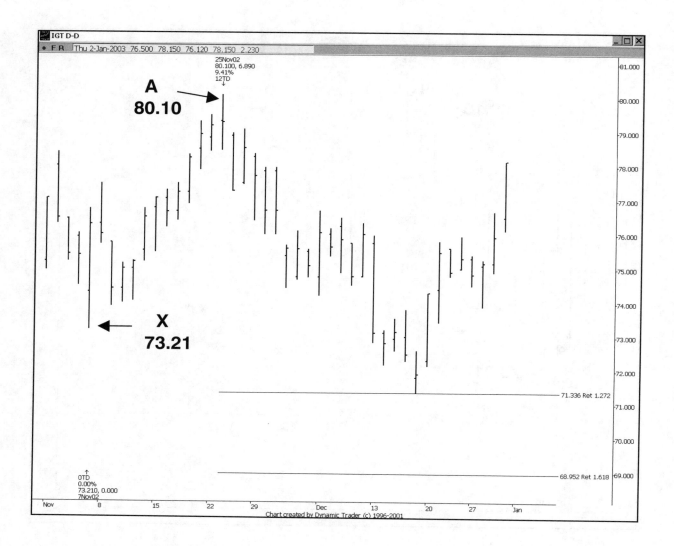

IGT traded down to the 1.272 extension level of swing X:A at 71.33 and did an immediate reversal and went up over 7 points in eight trading sessions.

Here is the same stock from a different perspective. Here we look to calculate resistance **extension** levels based on swing X:A.

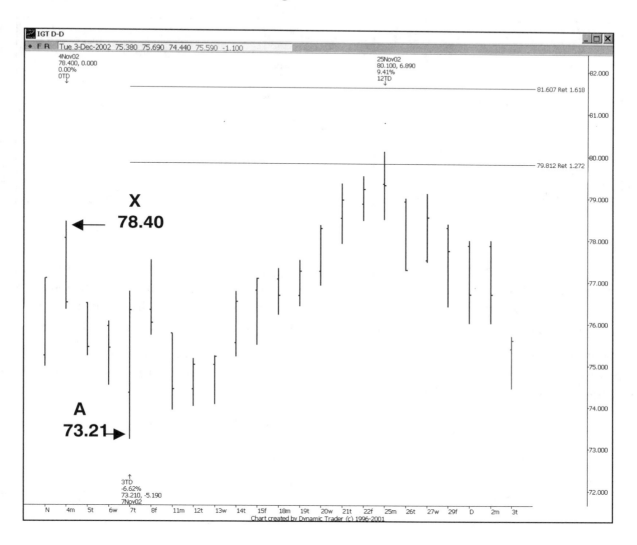

The daily chart of (IGT) above put in a swing high (X) at 78.40. Over the next 12 trading sessions (IGT) traded down to (A), which was a low of 73.21. A reversal to the upside began. So, as soon as the low (A) was established, we could calculate the Fibonacci extension levels that might act as resistance and stop the upside movement. Remember, extensions are basically retracements of greater than 100% of the X to A move. The specific ratios we use are 1.272 and 1.618. Those levels came in at:

$$1.272 = 79.81$$
$$1.618 = 81.60$$

## Projections

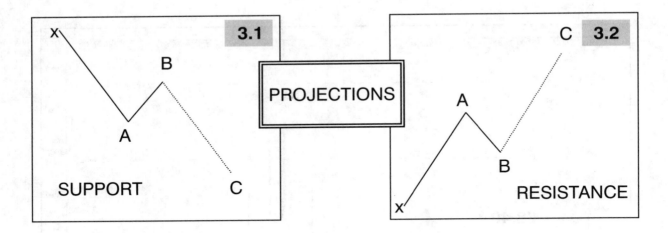

Now that we've covered retracements and extensions, the next Fibonacci study that I use is called a **projection**. From the figures above, projections measure the size of previous swings (X:A) in the same direction and project those swings from the current swing beginning at (B). The ratios used in this study are .618, 1.00, and 1.618.

Projections can be used to calculate support or resistance. To calculate a projection three points must already be established (X, A, B). For illustration purposes, let's assume X = 40, A = 30, B = 35.

First, let's calculate what the range of X to A is:

Price @ A: $30
Price @ X: $40

Range = $10

Next let's multiply this range by each Fibonacci ratio:

| Ratio | Points |
|---|---|
| 0.618 | $ 6.18 |
| 1.000 | $ 10.00 |
| 1.618 | $ 16.18 |

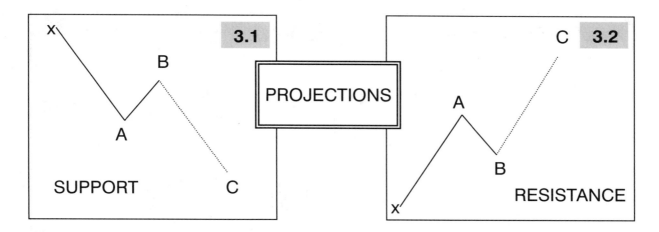

Finally, take the number from each ratio and subtract it from B, which is $35.00. This will provide you with Fibonacci projection levels:

| Ratio | Points | Pt. B | Fibonacci Projection Levels |
|-------|--------|-------|------------------------------|
| 0.618 | $ 6.18 | $ 35.00 | $ 28.82 |
| 1.000 | $ 10.00 | $ 35.00 | $ 25.00 |
| 1.618 | $ 16.18 | $ 35.00 | $ 18.82 |

So, if I were to ask you for the 1.618 projection of swing X:A from B, the answer would be $18.82. The price levels in the table above represent Fibonacci price support decisions. The exact same analysis can be done for Figure 3.2 to calculate projection levels acting as resistance. In Figure 3.2, X is $30, A is $40, B is $35. This time instead of subtracting from point B, we would add to B to determine price resistance levels:

| Ratio | Points | Pt. B | Fibonacci Projection Levels |
|-------|--------|-------|------------------------------|
| 0.618 | $ 6.16 | $ 35.00 | $ 41.16 |
| 1.000 | $ 10.00 | $ 35.00 | $ 45.00 |
| 1.618 | $ 16.18 | $ 35.00 | $ 51.18 |

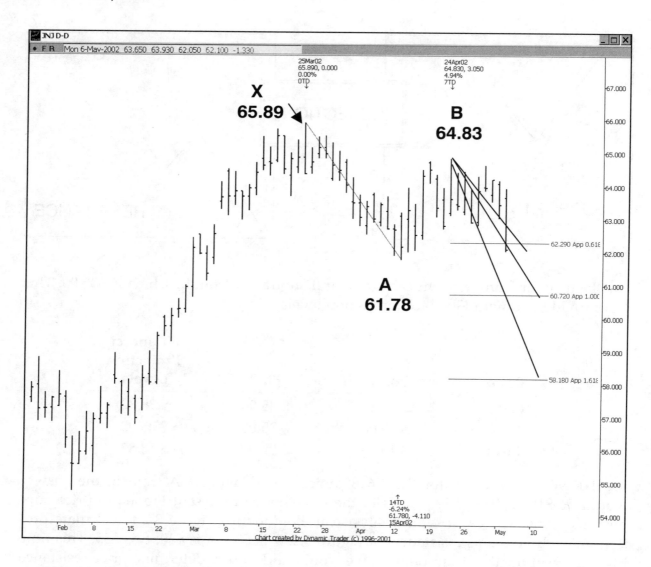

Above is an example of a price projection on the daily chart of Johnson & Johnson (JNJ). Swing X to A was measured for a total of 4.11 points. This range was multiplied by our Fibonacci ratios (.618, 1.00, 1.618) and each of the those numbers where then subtracted from swing B high of 64.83 to get the following projection support numbers:

$$.618 = 62.29$$
$$1.000 = 60.72$$
$$1.618 = 58.18$$

Above is an example of a price projection on the daily chart of (QSFT). Swing X to A was measured for a total of 8.4 points. This range was multiplied by our Fibonacci ratios (.618, 1.00, 1.618) and each of the those numbers were then added to swing B low of 13.24 to get the following projection resistance numbers:

.618 = 18.43
1.000 = 21.64
1.618 = 26.83

## Expansions

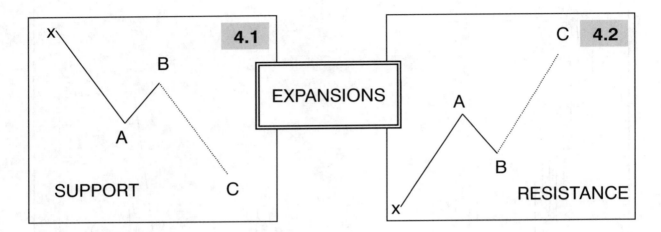

Price **expansions** are similar to projections with one small difference. Instead of measuring swing X:A and projecting it from B, we project the values from A. B is not used in this study. Basically, expansions measuring swing X:A "expand" that swing further in the direction price is headed using the following Fibonacci ratios: .618, 1.00, and 1.618. These price levels will be labeled as (Exp) on the charts.

To calculate an expansion only two points must be established (X, A). For illustration purposes, let's say X is 50 and A is 45 in Figure 4.1.

First, let's calculate what the range of X to A is:

Price @ A: $45
Price @ X: $50

Range = $5.00

Next let's multiply this range by each Fibonacci ratio:

| Ratio | Points |
|-------|--------|
| 0.618 | $ 3.09 |
| 1.000 | $ 5.00 |
| 1.618 | $ 8.09 |

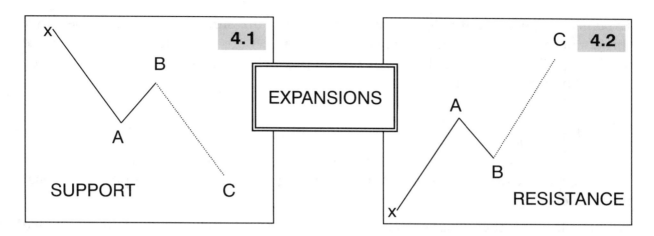

Finally, take the number from each ratio and subtract it from A, which is $35.00. This will provide you with Fibonacci projection levels:

| Ratio | Points | Pt. A | Fibonacci Expansion Level |
|---|---|---|---|
| 0.618 | $ 3.09 | $ 45.00 | $ 41.91 |
| 1.000 | $ 5.00 | $ 45.00 | $ 40.00 |
| 1.618 | $ 8.09 | $ 35.00 | $ 36.91 |

So, if I were to ask you for the 0.618 expansion of swing X:A, the answer would be $41.91. The price levels in the table above represent Fibonacci price support decisions. The exact same analysis can be done for Figure 4.2 to calculate projection levels acting as resistance. In Figure 4.2, X is $30, and A is $40. This time instead of subtracting from A we would add to A, to determine price resistance levels:

| Ratio | Points | Pt. A | Fibonacci Expansion Level |
|---|---|---|---|
| 0.618 | $ 6.18 | $ 40.00 | $ 46.18 |
| 1.000 | $ 10.00 | $ 40.00 | $ 50.00 |
| 1.618 | $ 16.18 | $ 40.00 | $ 56.18 |

Expansions are a "confirming" Fibonacci study. This simply means that the other three studies—retracements, extensions, and projections—should be the first price studies applied to a chart. Then utilize this price study to confirm a potential price support or resistance zone.

## REVIEW

In this chapter we learned general guidelines on how to spot significant highs and lows on a chart that will assist us in calculating Fibonacci price support and resistance levels.

We also learned the specific Fibonacci ratios used in each of the following price studies and how to calculate each of these Fibonacci price studies:

- Retracements
- Extensions
- Projections
- Expansions

Mastering these price studies will be essential to your success with the strategies in this book. It is imperative to be able to pull up a blank chart and calculate the Fibonacci price levels. It is through these Fibonacci price studies where areas of concentrated price levels will begin to appear. Those concentrated zones are the focus of the next chapter.

CHAPTER **3**

# USING FIBZONES TO IDENTIFY HIGH-PROBABILITY REVERSALS

# WHAT IS A FIBZONE?

Now that we have reviewed the various methods to create Fibonacci price levels, it is time to shift gears from theory into strategy. Almost all of the strategies I trade are based on a stock, commodity, or futures contract hitting a Fibonacci price support or resistance zone. I have coined the phrase "FibZone" to represent these areas. Below is the definition of a FibZone.

**FibZone:** A relatively tight range of price where a confluence of any combination of at least three Fibonacci price retracements, extensions, projections, or expansions occur. If a FibZone occurs above the current price, it is resistance, and if a FibZone is below the current price, it is support. I have coined a unique phrase to describe a not-so-unique general concept. What I call a FibZone, others call "confluence," "price zones," "clusters," etc. Later, you will find that I have defined specific types of FibZones that do carry a unique and different characteristic to the run-of-the-mill "zone." Below is a perfect example of a Support FibZone.

Let's walk through an example of how to build a FibZone. Below is a daily chart of AOL. Price has just made a swing high point on December 2, 2002. The goal now is to create one or multiple Support FibZones where AOL will likely stop declining and reverse up to continue the current uptrend. To do that, the first step is to identify the key high and low points.

## STEP #1: Identify Key High and Low Points

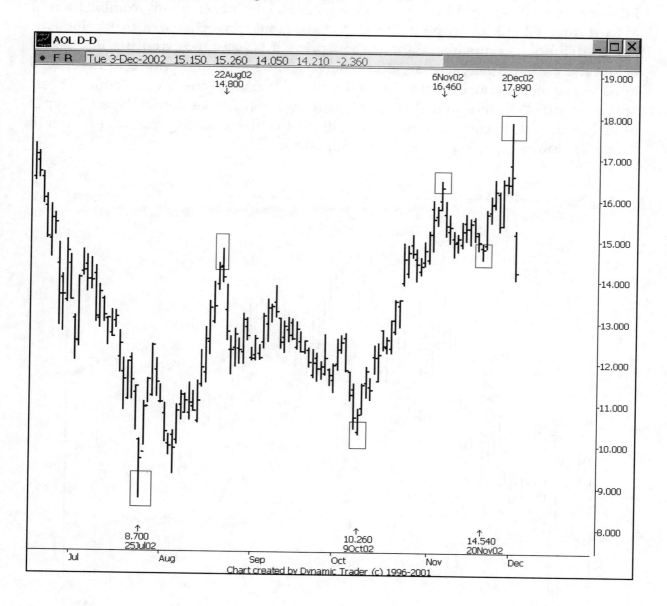

Now that the key points are determined, we can begin to apply our Fibonacci price studies. The first Fibonacci price study to apply is a retracement. So, let's measure from the July 2002 low to the December 2002 high and calculate the various retracement levels. If the current price on the chart is already below a retracement level, then delete the Fibonacci price level, as it has been "violated" and is no longer a valid support level.

## STEP #2: Calculate RETRACEMENT levels using swing low points identified in this uptrend and the current swing high point.

(Swing Points:  Low = 8.70      High = 17.89)

This is a continuation of Step #2, as we have a higher swing low point we will use to calculate additional retracement levels using the October 9 low of 10.26 and the December 2 high of 17.89. As you can see, there are now a couple of price levels starting to group together. A zone is beginning to form.

## STEP #2 (cont.): Calculate RETRACEMENT levels using swing low points identified in this uptrend.

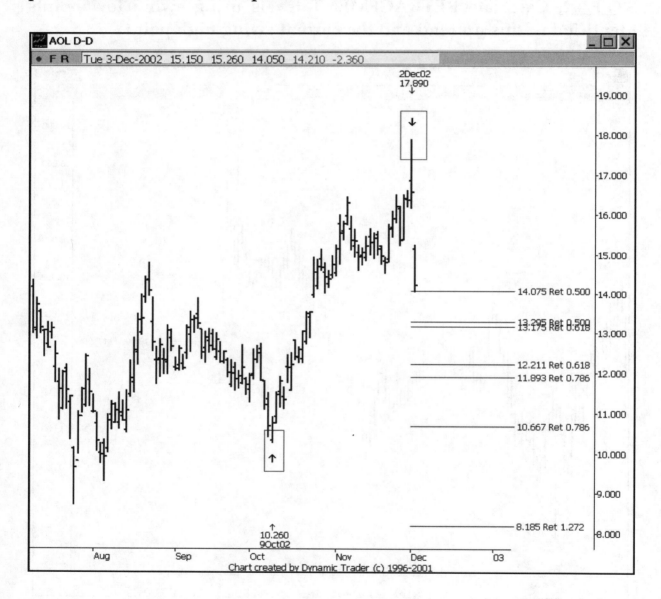

(Swing Points:    Low = 10.26    High = 17.89)

Now let's shift to calculating extension levels. Remember, an extension is simply a retracement greater than 100%. So, with the low point from November 20 at a higher level than the current price, I am concerned with the 1.272 and 1.618 extension levels that come in at 13.62 and 12.47, respectively. Can you see a zone forming?

**STEP #3: Calculate EXTENSION levels using swing low points that are higher than current price up to the current swing high.**

(Swing Points:   Low = 14.54   High = 17.89)

Now let's apply a Projection study. In this trend up, there has been one countertrend decline from August 22 to October 9 that was 4.5 points. Project this decline from the current December 2 swing high point of 17.89. This simply means subtract 4.5 points from 17.89 and we have a projection or "symmetry" level at 13.39.

**<u>STEP #4</u>: Calculate PROJECTION levels by measuring previous declines (in an uptrend) and subtract the size of those declines from the current high point. Opposite for downtrends.**

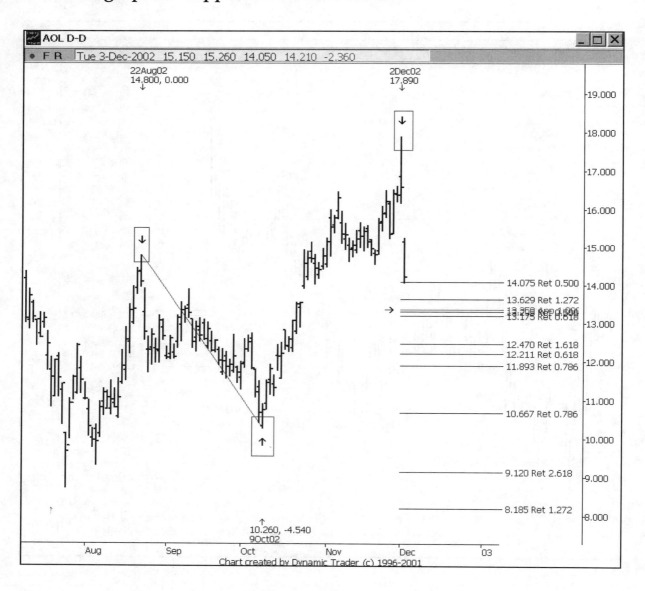

(Swing Points:    High: 14.80    Low = 10.26    High = 17.89)

## IDENTIFYING A FIBZONE

Here is your new Support FibZone that will be used to look for long trades. Note that due to the nature of this chart, we did not need to calculate EXPANSION levels. If this study can be performed, it should be done after the retracements, extensions, and projections have been calculated.

You will notice that the range of the FibZone in the chart below is spanning a 2 point range. How does this provide you with an edge? The key is to remember that you should never trade on the basis of a FibZone alone. You should only trade when you have a legitimate entry pattern within the FibZone. This applies no matter how many Fibonacci levels are calculated for a specific price level. I apply several different entry patterns to the Fibonacci strategies that you will learn in this book. I will teach them to you in Chapter 11.

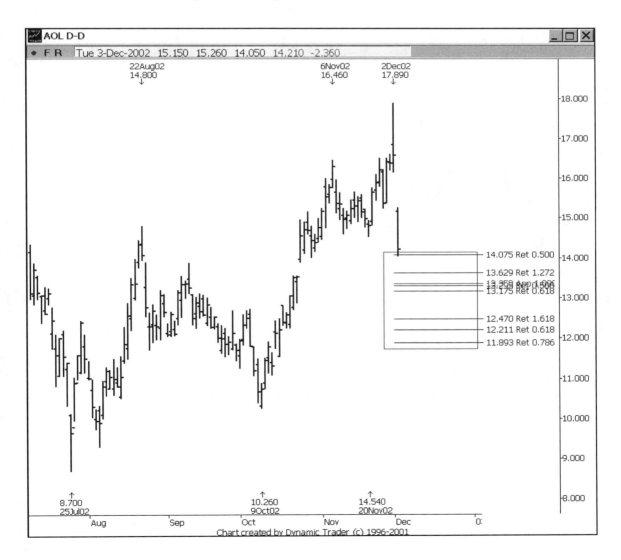

Just to play out this example, AOL traded deep into our Support FibZone, but reversed around 12.20 and rallied up to almost $16.00 over a couple of weeks of activity. This would have been a 27% gain for someone who identified an entry pattern within a Support FibZone.

## STRATEGY Q&A

*Question:* Does the size of the FibZone matter?

*Answer:* To qualify as a zone, it needs at least three Fibonacci price levels. Yes, as the number of price levels that occur in a FibZone increase, the more important that FibZone becomes. I equate it to ripping one piece of paper in half or trying to rip a phone book in half. One page is no problem. But as each additional page is added to the stack, it becomes more difficult to tear them in half.

*Question:* What Fibonacci ratio is the most important in a FibZone?

*Answer:* A couple of the strategies I discuss have specific ratios that must be present. These are specific types of FibZones. Generally speaking, though, I am not looking for a specific ratio. I just want to see a confluence of Fibonacci price levels (I don't care which ones) in a relatively tight range.

*Question:* Which Fibonacci studies are better?

*Answer:* Well, as you have read, there are four basic Fibonacci studies: Retracements, Extensions, Projections, and Expansions. No study is necessarily better than another. I continue to go back to the focus of the FibZone. A tight price area with a large number of price levels represents a trading opportunity.

*Question:* After running the Fibonacci studies on a chart, do you remove any of the Fibonacci levels from the chart?

*Answer:* Yes. If a price level is hanging out all by itself on the chart with no other Fibonacci levels around it to create a FibZone, then I will delete that price level. I am simply looking for groups of Fibonacci ratios concentrated in a small price range.

*Question:* How big can a FibZone be?

*Answer:* Depending on the chart, a FibZone can be very wide. However, for trading purposes, I try to find charts that provide FibZones that are no more than 10% of the price of the security from the low price to the high price of the zone. Many times the zone is closer to 5% in the width of the price of the stock or commodity. For example, I wouldn't want a FibZone on a $40 stock to be much more than 4 points deep.

**Question:** *Sometimes there is more than one zone after running these studies. So, how do you decide which one to trade against?*

**Answer:** FibZones simply provide decision points in a particular market. A **decision point,** that's it. Fibonacci, by definition, is a tool that assists the trader in finding support and resistance levels. So, the key to knowing what zone to trade against will be based on what you use for a "trigger." After those decision zones are on the chart, it is necessary to have certain patterns, indicators, oscillators, etc., that you will use to determine the internals of the market you are looking at and when to actually take a trade. That will be the focus of most of the rest of this book.

**Question:** *What software programs do you recommend using to calculate these FibZones?*

**Answer:** There seems to be a new software program coming out every day to address Fibonacci. I personally use Dynamic Trader. I believe it is the most comprehensive Fibonacci tool on the market right now. Whatever program you consider, I think you need to be able to delete lines/price levels that you don't need, be able to do each study we mentioned earlier, and manipulate the chart with relative ease, as well as perform other technical studies, and the ability to make notes on the charts. I personally also require a program that allows me to convert a bar chart to candlesticks.

**Question:** *When is a zone recalculated?*

**Answer:** In an uptrend, a new support zone is calculated when the current high is violated and a new high point is made. In a downtrend, a new resistance zone is calculated when the current swing low point is violated and a new lower low point is made. Remember, a high point is confirmed when a lower high is made on each side of the high, and a low point is confirmed when a higher low is made on each side.

# SECTION II

# MY FAVORITE FIBONACCI STRATEGIES

# SPECIAL NOTE BEFORE I TEACH YOU MY FIBONACCI TRADING STRATEGIES

**B**efore I begin teaching you my trading strategies in the following chapters, I want to state emphatically that you must always wait for confirmation before taking a trade. That means you wait for a trigger before entering a long or short position. All of the strategies we'll be discussing involve a stock hitting a FibZone, and it is in the price action against this FibZone where I look for entries.

After we walk through all the strategies, I will follow up with a discussion and list of the pattern triggers I use to enter trades in Chapter 11.

For the purposes of this book, please make these two assumptions:

1. Always use a pattern or some other form of trigger to enter a trade.

2. Whenever I refer to entries as I teach you my strategies, I am referring to one of the patterns in Chapter 11.

CHAPTER **4**

# HOW TO ENTER TRENDS USING THE TREND TRIGGER STRATEGY

# STRATEGY #1: TREND TRIGGER

Trend Trigger is probably the simplest way to trade with FibZones. The basic assumption here is that we are trading with the trend and that a normal and natural pullback is occurring, and this pullback will stop somewhere in our FibZone and reverse direction.

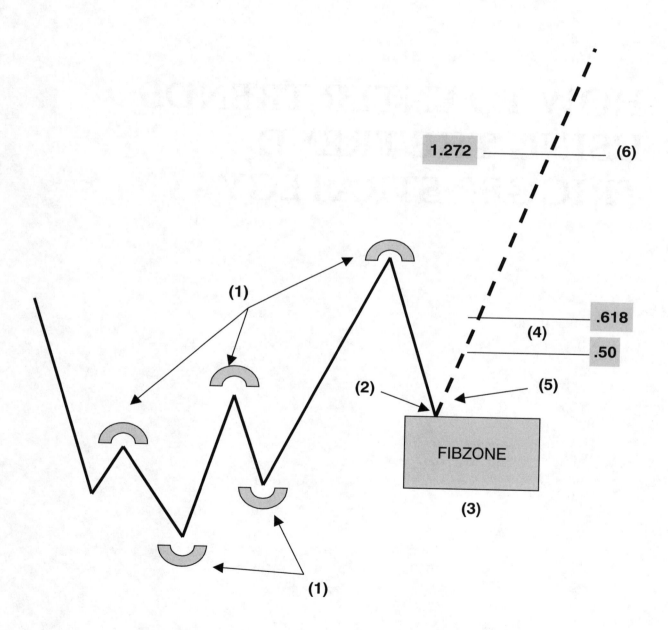

## Rules For Buys (Sells Are Reversed)

1.  There must be at least two higher swing high points and at least one higher swing low point. This structurally confirms we are trading with the immediate trend.

2.  The current bar low must at least touch the top of the FibZone. At this point, look for an entry pattern to get you into the trade.

3.  Once you are filled, a stop loss order should be placed just below the FibZone. This assumes your money management rules will allow you to risk the entire zone. If not, do not take the trade until price drops deep enough into the zone to meet your money management stop loss rules, or reduce the number of shares or contracts to be purchased.

4.  Once a swing low point is determined against the FibZone, calculate the .50, .618, and 1.272 extension of the high-to-low swing into the Support FibZone. These levels will serve as profit objectives.

5.  The first profit-taking area is between the .50 and .618 retracement range. Once these profits are booked, trail your stop loss to reduce risk.

6.  The final objective of a Trend Trigger trade is the 1.272 extension of the high-to-low swing made into our FibZone.

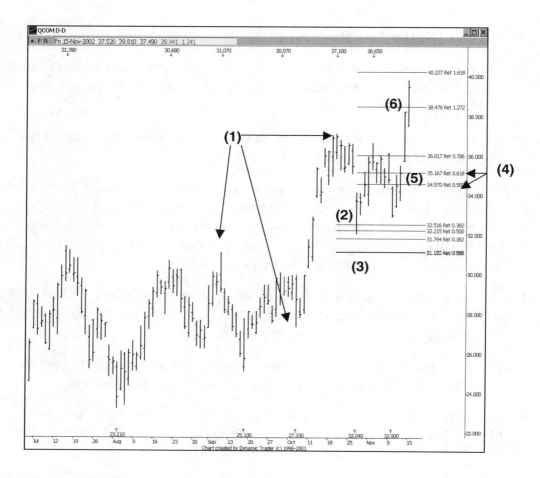

## Trend Trigger Example: Long

1. We have identified two higher swing high points with at least one higher swing low point.

2. Price touches the Support FibZone, and I'm long at 32.60 based on the trigger I use.

3. The initial stop is placed just below the zone around 31.00.

4. With a swing low in place, we calculate the .50 and .618 retracement levels of the high-to-low swing into support.

5. Profits are taken on half the position between 34.57 and 35.16, which are the .50 and .618 retracement levels. At this point, I also move my stop to breakeven.

6. The final objective on the trade is 38.47, which is the 1.272 extension of the high-to-low swing into the Support FibZone.

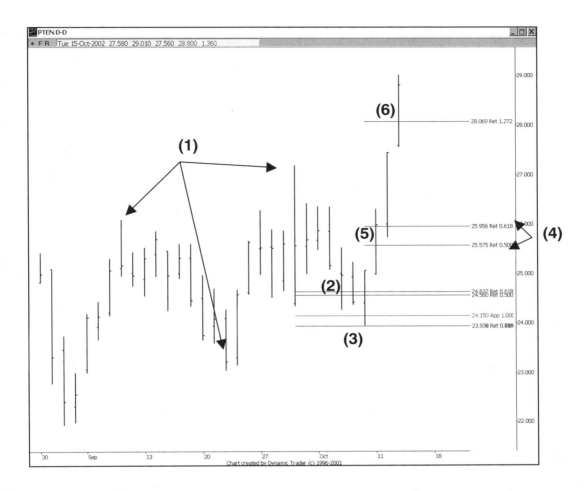

## Trend Trigger Example: Long

1. We identify two higher swing high points and a higher swing low point.

2. After making a swing high, price comes down and touches our zone at 24.63, which is where we take a long position.

3. Our initial stop loss order is placed just below the zone around 23.80.

4. Price goes lower into the zone over the next couple of days, then reverses up out of the FibZone. We calculate the .50 and .618 retracement of the high-to-low swing into support.

5. I take partial profits between 25.57 and 26.00 and immediately trail my stop to reduce risk.

6. The final objective, which is the 1.272 extension of the high-to-low swing into support, is hit and I take the last portion of the long off around 28.06.

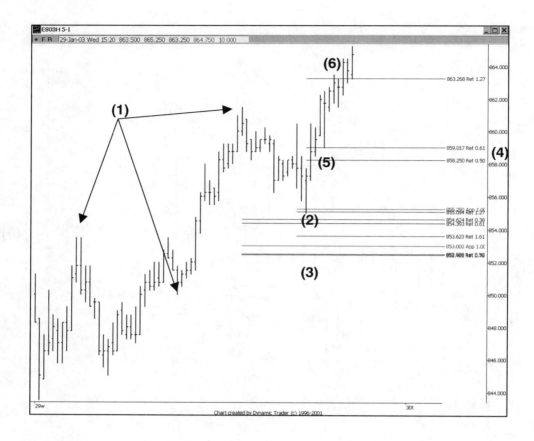

## Trend Trigger Example: Long

I've found the Trend Trigger to be a great intraday trading strategy. Here's a great example.

1. Two higher swing highs and a higher swing low have been identified on this 5-minute chart. Once the second swing high is made, we can calculate price support. That zone comes in from 852.25–855.25.

2. Price comes down and touches the zone, so I go long at 855.25.

3. My stop is at 852. That's 3.25 points of risk.

4. Once a swing low is made into the zone, we can calculate the .50 and .618 retracement of the high-to-low swing into our Support FibZone. These price levels are 858.25 and 859.00.

5. Price hits our first target and half the position is taken off at 858.50. My stop is moved up to breakeven (especially on intraday trades).

6. The final objective at the 1.272 extension of the high-to-low swing into support is hit at 863.25.

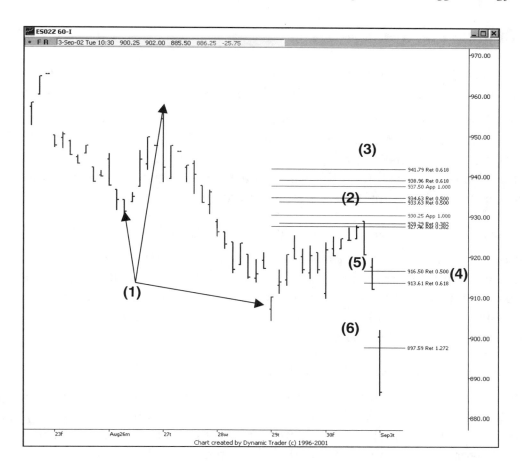

## Trend Trigger Example: Short

1. Two lower swing lows and at least one lower swing high have been identified. Once the second swing low is made, we can calculate price resistance. That zone comes in from 927.50–941.75.

2. Price rallies up and touches the Resistance FibZone, so I go short at 927.50.

3. My stop is at 942.00. That's 14.5 points of risk.

4. Once a swing high is made into the FibZone, we can calculate the .50 and .618 retracement of the low-to-high swing into our Resistance FibZone. These price levels are 916.50 and 913.50.

5. Price hits our first target and half the position is taken off around 916.00. My stop is moved down to breakeven (especially on intraday trades).

6. The final objective at the 1.272 extension of the low-to-high swing into resistance is hit at 897.50.

## STRATEGY Q&A

*Question: What if a Trend Trigger trade comes up and the FibZone is too large and I am unable to put a stop below the FibZone and risk that much?*

*Answer:* Don't take the trade until the stock drops lower into the FibZone (for longs). If your money management rules don't allow you to take the trade, then please don't take it. Risking too much on one trade will come back to haunt you. The other choice is to still take the trade, but trade fewer shares or contracts to keep your risk in line with your money management rules.

*Question: Where do you place the stop after hitting the first objective?*

*Answer:* Ideally a stop can be placed at your original entry price so that risk can be completely eliminated from the trade. However, there are situations where moving the stops to that level will get you prematurely stopped out of the trade. Be aware of the volatility of the stock, and avoid placing stops at round numbers or levels too close to the current market price.

*Question: How long do you typically hold these trades?*

*Answer:* That is always dictated by the market. It has been my observation that the best trades bounce immediately out of a FibZone and become profitable quickly. If I find myself looking at a chart where price has hit our zone and it continues to print bars that hover around the FibZone, then I often scratch the trade.

*Question: Are there any confirming indicators to use with this strategy?*

*Answer:* By definition, this is supposed to be a "trend following" strategy. We are trying to identify pullbacks into FibZones. So, the stronger the trend, the better the opportunity. I've found that a strong ADX reading is an excellent scanning tool, as well as a nice confirming indicator. I would use a 14-period ADX of 20 or greater. Ideally, the ADX line is upsloping and not downsloping. This just means the reading is continuing to go higher and the trend is getting stronger. Downsloping means the trend is losing strength.

CHAPTER **5**

# THE REFLECTION
# REVERSAL METHOD

Here is a strategy that should lay to rest any doubt you may have about order in the markets.

Reflection is a strategy that combines three concepts with our FibZones. Those concepts are **Symmetry, Average Directional Index (ADX),** and **Directional Indicator (DI).** Let's quickly review each of these concepts. After our review, we will look at a few examples of Reflection in action.

**Symmetry:** When the current market swing is similar in relation to price and/or time with the previous market swing. With this kind of similarity, or symmetry, there is a high likelihood for price to reverse direction. Let's look at a couple of examples.

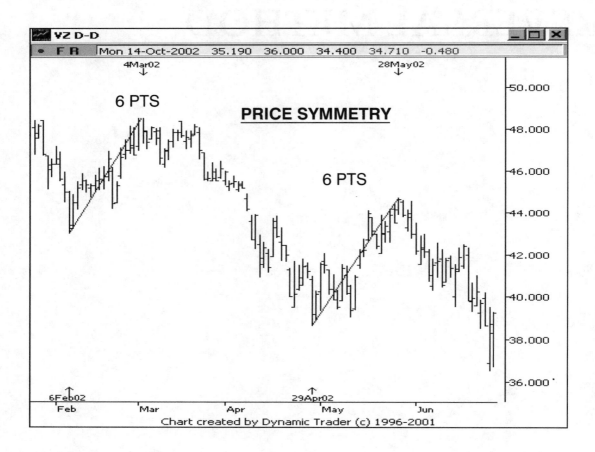

Above is a daily chart of Verizon Wireless (VZ). This illustrates the power of price symmetry. After VZ completed a 6 point rally on May 28, 2002, which matched the previous rally that ended March 4, 2002, VZ sells off more than 7 points over a few weeks with very little countertrend movement.

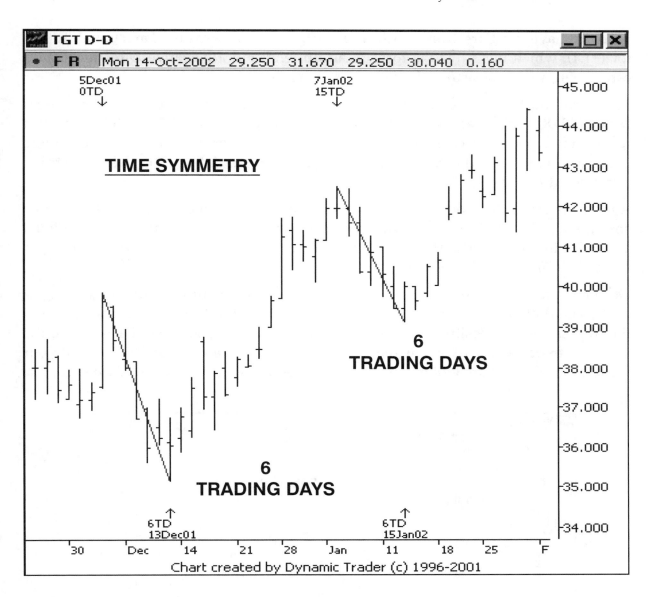

Symmetry, in the markets, not only exists on the price axis, but also on the time axis. Symmetry that occurs on the time axis can be a precursor to powerful reversals as well. The illustration above is a daily chart of the retailer Target (TGT). On January 15, 2002, the market had just completed a six-day selloff from high to low. Coincidentally (or not), the previous countertrend decline was also six days. After the January 15 low was put in, the stock climbed over 5 points in a few days. That's over 10% in one week's time.

Next we have the **Directional Indicator (DI).** There is a Positive Directional Indicator (+DI), which measures the force of an uptrend and a Negative Directional Indicator (–DI), which measures the force of a downtrend.

The third and final ingredient to our Reflection strategy is the **Average Directional Index (ADX).** This is an oscillator that moves between 0 and 100 and tells the chart reader how strong the current trend is, but NOT whether that trend is up or down. Readings below 20 indicate a weak trend and readings above 35 represent a strong trend. Readings above 60 are rare.

Again, the ADX does not tell you the direction of the trend, it simply states how strong a trend is, be it up or down. Most charting software packages combine the DI and ADX into one study. The DI and ADX originate from Welles Wilder's book *New Concepts In Technical Trading Systems* written in 1978.

On the chart of Verizon (VZ) below, I have added the DI study to the bottom of the chart. The dotted line represents a Negative Directional Indicator (–DI) and the solid line represents the Positive Directional Indicator (+DI). When the –DI is above the +DI, the trend is down. When the +DI is above the –DI, the trend is up. For our study purposes, we are looking at the Directional Indicator of the past 21 bars.

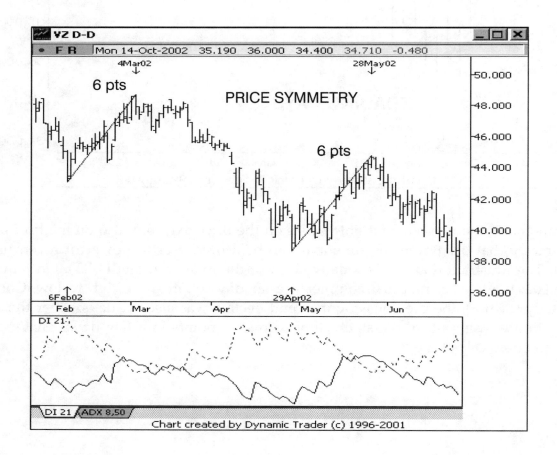

Below is a chart with the ADX study at the bottom. In our studies, we will be using an eight-period ADX with our reference line at 50. As mentioned earlier, a reading of 35 signifies a strong trend. ADX readings of 50 and 60 are rare and typically represent a short-term blow-off in the trend.

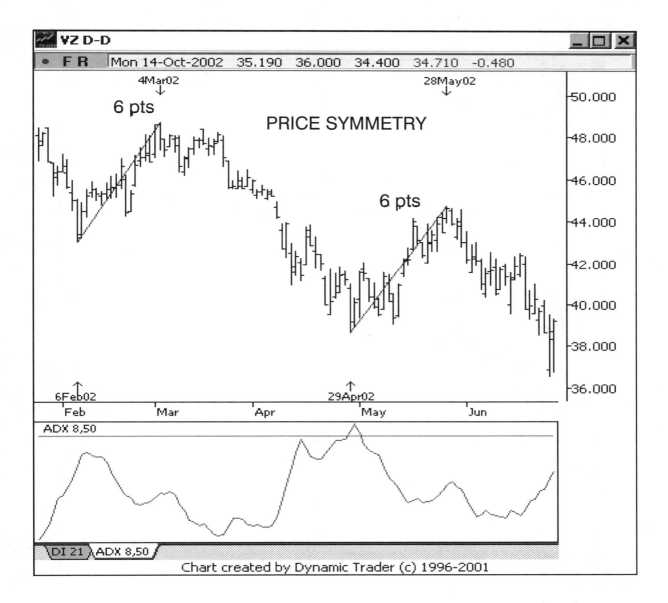

Let's summarize. For the Reflection strategy, we will be looking at **Symmetry, Directional Indicator,** and **Average Directional Index** against our FibZones. Now that we have established what each ingredient looks like, let me teach you the rules for long and short trades.

# STRATEGY #2: REFLECTION

The goal with this strategy is to find strong short- to intermediate-term trends using the ADX and DI that are in the process of pulling back into a FibZone. The kicker here is that we are looking for the pullback to be symmetrical in time or price with the previous countertrend swing. It is this symmetry that triggers powerful reversals.

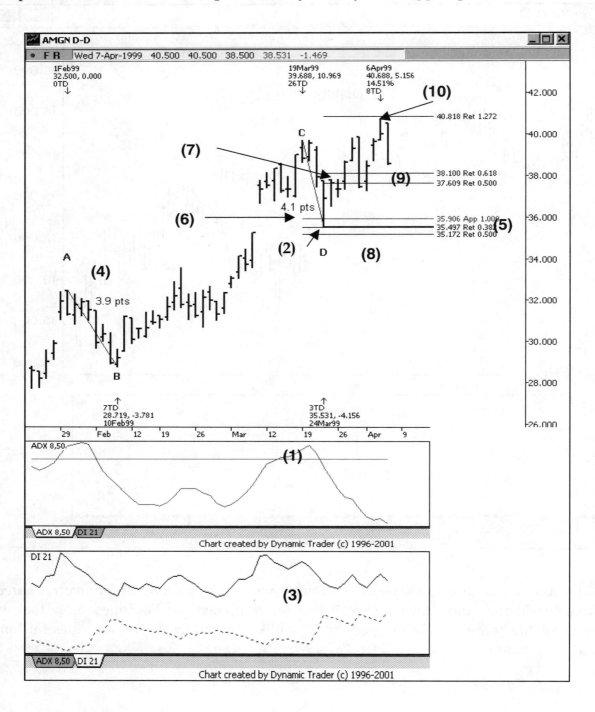

*Note: In other chapters, I illustrate strategies using a diagram. Due to the combination of indicators that the Reflection Strategy uses, I will use an actual chart (shown on the previous page) of real price action instead.*

## Rules For Buys (Shorts Are Reversed):

1. The eight-period ADX must cross above 50.

2. After #1 is complete, wait for a swing high point to form. This swing point will be labeled "C."

3. At swing point "C," the 21-period DI should show the +DI line above the –DI line. Between the ADX and +DI, this will give us a stock that is strongly trending and is trending up based on the +DI oscillator reading.

4. After items 1 through 3 have been established, from point C, find the previous significant countertrend decline. Measure the amount of time that countertrend lasted and the number of points it declined from high to low. The high point will be labeled A, and the low point of this countertrend rally will be labeled B.

5. Using retracements, extensions, projections, and expansions, calculate Fibonacci price support levels based on the high point C.

6. One addition that we will add to our normal Fibonacci analysis is measuring the size of Swing A:B from #4 and projecting that price rally from swing high point C. This will establish the price symmetry point and help us to focus on a specific Support FibZone to look for a trade against.

7. Once price hits our Support FibZone, look to buy on a trade above the previous day's high.

8. The initial stop will be just below the Support FibZone.

9. The first objective on this trade is between the .50 and .618 retracement of high point C to low point D made into our Support FibZone. At this point, trail the stop to breakeven, or as close to breakeven as you can get based on the price action.

10. The final objective is the 1.272 extension of high point C to low point D made into the Support FibZone.

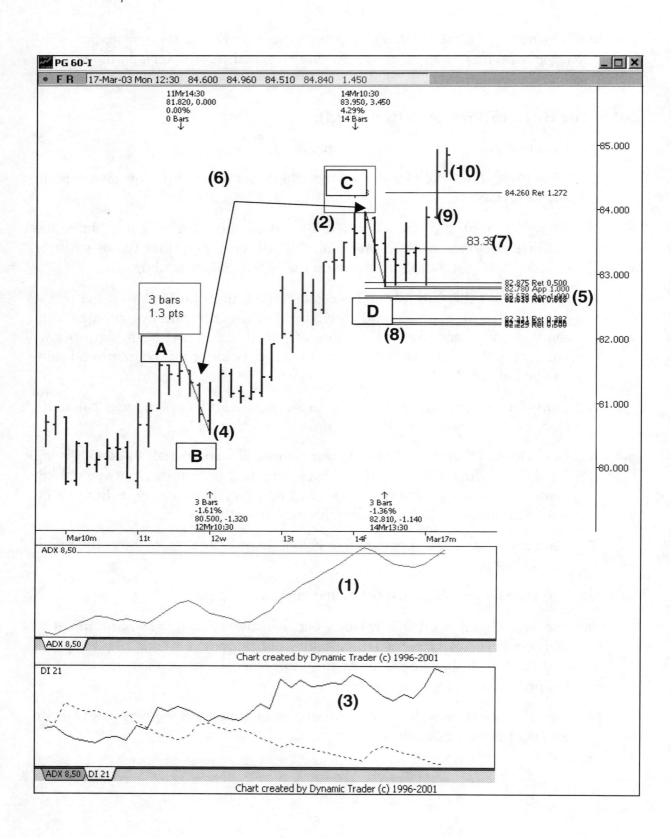

Chart created by Dynamic Trader (c) 1996-2001

## Reflection Long Example

1. The eight-period ADX crosses above 50.

2. A swing high point is formed just under $84. This point will be labeled point C.

3. At point C, confirm that the 21-period +DI is above the –DI line. In this case, it is, so we can continue with the setup.

4. Now go back to the previous countertrend decline. It is labeled A:B with A being the high point. This countertrend move was three bars (each bar was 60 minutes) and a total of 1.3 points. We'll come back to this, but it is critical to identify the amount of time and the size of the previous decline.

5. With the high point in place, it is time to calculate Fibonacci price levels and construct a Support FibZone. This zone comes in from 82.22 to 82.87.

6. Remember our measurement from #4? Let's take that 1.3 point decline and project it from the point C high. That price level comes in at 82.78. This is called the Symmetry level, which happens to fall within our Support FibZone.

7. Price hits our FibZone and begins to reverse. A long trade is entered on a trade above the previous bar's high AFTER hitting the Support FibZone. Our entry in this scenario was 83.39.

8. A stop is placed immediately below the Support FibZone.

9. Once price starts to reverse to the upside, we can label the low point into the Support FibZone as point D. Now we can calculate the .50 and .618 retracement of the move from C to D. This is typically where we take partial profits and trail up our stop. However, this is a scenario that often occurs on lower time frames where there really isn't a gain to lock in at this point, so I do not take any profits there. I wait to take the entire position off at the 1.272. The only action item here would be to trail the stop to higher levels, ideally to breakeven, or to the swing low point made into the Support FibZone.

10. The final objective, which is the 1.272 extension of swing C:D, is hit at 84.26 for an approximately 1 point gain in three hours of trading. Note that an optional money management technique once the 1.272 level is hit would be to trail the stop to the previous bar's low. That way it allows you to potentially participate in a much larger move, if it develops. The downside is that you could give up gains as well, but it does keep you in a winning trade.

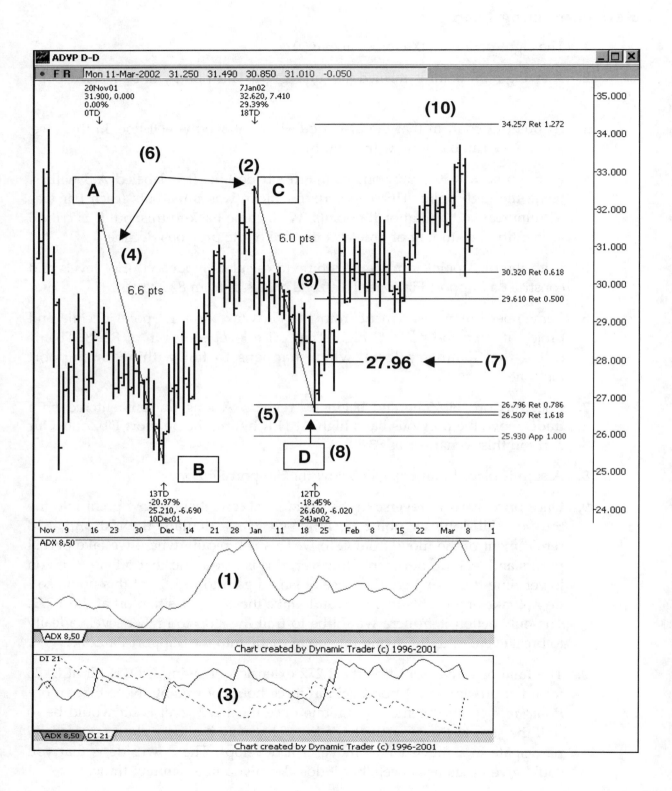

## Reflection Long Example

1.  The eight-period ADX crosses above 50.

2.  A swing high point is formed just under $32.62. This point will be labeled point C.

3.  At point C, confirm that the 21-period +DI is above the –DI line. In this case it is, so we can continue with the setup.

4.  Now go back to the previous countertrend decline. It is labeled A:B with A being the high point. This countertrend move was 13 days and a total of 6.6 points. We'll come back to this, but it is critical to identify the amount of time and size of the previous decline.

5.  With high point C in place, it is time to calculate Fibonacci price levels and construct a Support FibZone. This zone comes in from 25.93 to 26.79.

6.  Remember our measurement from #4? Let's take that 6.6 point decline and project it from the point C high. That price level comes in at 25.93. This is called the Symmetry level, which happens to fall around our Support FibZone.

7.  Price hits our FibZone and begins to reverse. Note that the reversal begins on day 12. The previous decline was 13 days. So we have symmetry of time as well. This only strengthens the reversal. A long trade is entered above the previous bar's high AFTER hitting the Support FibZone. Our entry in this scenario was 27.96.

8.  A stop is placed immediately below the Support FibZone.

9.  Once price starts to reverse to the upside, we can label the low point into the Support FibZone as point D. Now we can calculate the .50 and .618 retracement of the move from C to D. Those price levels are 29.61 and 30.32. One trading session after entering this trade, the first objective zone is hit and we take profits on half the trade. Now we move the stop on the remaining position either to breakeven or to the swing low point made into the Support FibZone. Had you moved it to breakeven, you would have been stopped out on the remaining position. I prefer to keep my stops below/above price structure or swing points, not based on my personal breakeven. The market could care less about my breakeven point.

10. We get within .50 of the final objective and begin to reverse. When I get close to my objective like this, my stops get very tight. For example, in this scenario why risk two or three dollars to capture .50? Regardless, we pulled out about 5 points of profits off of this setup. Not too shabby.

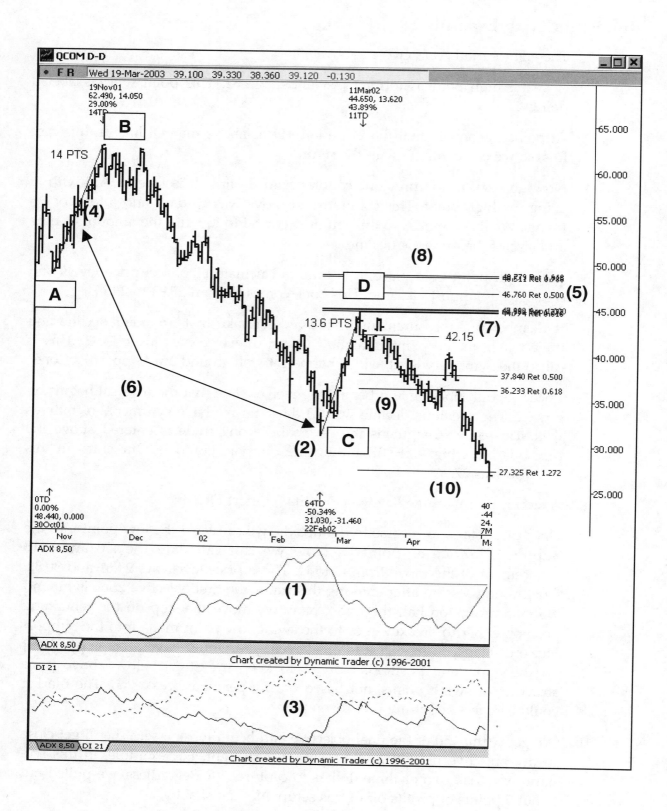

QCOM D-D

• F R   Wed 19-Mar-2003   39.100   39.330   38.360   39.120   -0.130

19Nov01
62.490, 14.050
29.00%
14TD

11Mar02
44.650, 13.620
43.89%
11TD
↓

**B**

14 PTS

**(4)**

**A**

**(6)**

**(8)**

**D**

48.877 Ret 0.948

46.760 Ret 0.500   **(5)**

44.994 Ret 0.618

13.6 PTS

**(7)**

42.15

37.840 Ret 0.500

36.233 Ret 0.618

**(9)**

**(2)**   **C**

27.325 Ret 1.272

**(10)**

65.000

60.000

55.000

50.000

45.000

40.000

35.000

30.000

25.000

0TD
0.00%
48.440, 0.000
30Oct01

64TD
-50.34%
31.030, -31.460
22Feb02

40°
-44
24.
7M

Nov        Dec        02        Feb        Mar        Apr        Ma

ADX 8,50

**(1)**

ADX 8,50

Chart created by Dynamic Trader (c) 1996-2001

DI 21

**(3)**

ADX 8,50   DI 21

Chart created by Dynamic Trader (c) 1996-2001

*Now, referring to the chart on the previous page . . .*

## Rules For Shorts (Buys Are Reversed):

1.  The eight-period ADX must cross above 50.

2.  After #1 is complete, wait for a swing point low to form. This swing point will be labeled "C."

3.  At swing point "C" the 21-period DI should show the –DI line above the +DI line. Between the ADX and DI this will give us a stock that is strongly trending and is trending down based on the –DI oscillator reading.

4.  After items 1 through 3 have been established, from point C, find the previous significant countertrend rally. Measure the amount of time that countertrend lasted and the number of points it rallied from low to high. The low point will be labeled A, and the high point of this countertrend rally will be labeled B.

5.  Using retracements, extensions, projections, and expansions, calculate Fibonacci price resistance levels based on low point C.

6.  One addition that we will add to our normal Fibonacci analysis is measuring the size of Swing A:B from #4 and projecting that price rally from swing low point C. This will establish the price symmetry point and help us to focus on a specific Resistance FibZone to look for a trade against.

7.  Once price hits our Resistance FibZone, look to short on a trade below the previous day's low.

8.  The initial stop will be just above the Resistance FibZone.

9.  The first objective on this trade is between the .50 and .618 retracement of low point C to high point D made into our Resistance FibZone. At this point, trail the stop to breakeven, or as close to breakeven as you can get, based on price action.

10. The final objective is the 1.272 extension of low point C to high point D made into the Resistance FibZone.

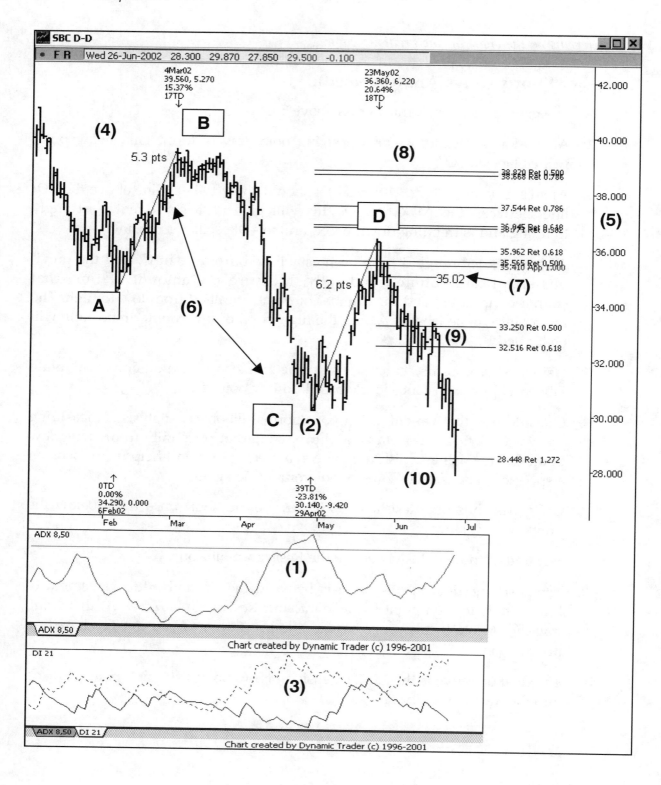

## Reflection Short Example

1.  The eight-period ADX crosses above 50.

2.  A swing low point is formed at 30.14. This point will be labeled point C.

3.  At point C, confirm that the 21-period –DI is above the +DI line. In this case it is, so we can continue with the setup.

4.  Now, go back to the previous countertrend rally of significance. Above it is labeled A:B, with A being the low point. This countertrend move was 17 days and 5.3 points. We'll come back to this, but it is critical to identify the amount of time and size of the previous rally.

5.  With the high point in place, it is time to calculate Fibonacci price levels and construct a Resistance FibZone. This zone comes in from 35.41 to 38.82.

6.  Remember our measurement from #4? Let's take that 5.3 point rally and project it from the point C low. That price level comes in right around $35.41. This is called the Symmetry level, which happens to fall right at our Resistance FibZone.

7.  Price hits our FibZone and begins to reverse. A short trade is entered on a trade below the previous bar's low AFTER hitting the Resistance FibZone. Our entry in this scenario was 35.02.

8.  A stop is placed immediately above the Resistance FibZone.

9.  Once price starts to reverse to the downside, we can label the high point into the Resistance FibZone as point D. Now we can calculate the .50 and .618 retracement of the move from C to D. This is where we take partial profits and trail our stop. So, half the position is covered around 33.00 for a 2 point gain and a stop is trailed down to either a previous swing high point or breakeven.

10. The final objective, which is the 1.272 extension of swing C:D, is hit at 28.44 for approximately a 6.5 point gain.

## STRATEGY Q&A

*Question:* Is there a mechanical way to scan for symmetry?

*Answer:* To my knowledge, there is no software that can scan for price symmetry. I do know that some software programs are working on perfecting the time symmetry scan. That's one of the reasons I like these strategies. They are not easily put into a box.

*Question:* Why do you take partial profits between the .50 and .618 retracement levels?

*Answer:* Trading this strategy, I found that stocks or commodities would reverse at this level and many times stop me out for a loss. When I started taking profits and trailing stops at this level, I not only added some "base hits" of profits to my bottom line, but I eliminated losses. Then occasionally I would hit a home run on the last half of a trade that kept moving in my direction. Sure, there are cases where I get stopped out prematurely and price keeps moving in the direction I wanted. That's trading!

CHAPTER **6**

# TRADING PULLBACKS USING THE TRIPLE CROWN STRATEGY

# STRATEGY #3: TRIPLE CROWN

After analyzing thousands upon thousands of Support and Resistance FibZones and analyzing what the characteristics were of those FibZones that provided some of the most powerful trading opportunities, I have found a combination of Fibonacci price levels based on a specific set of swing high and low points that are combined to create what is one of my favorite strategies, the Triple Crown. A Triple Crown is comprised of three Fibonacci price ratios which occur in this specific order:

.50

.786

.618

It is a specific combination of these three Fibonacci retracement levels that identify potentially powerful reversal areas in any tradable market with liquidity.

There are three swing points that we need to be concerned with in this strategy from which the ratios are derived. In the case of looking for long trades, we identify the most recent swing high point and the two most recent swing low points.

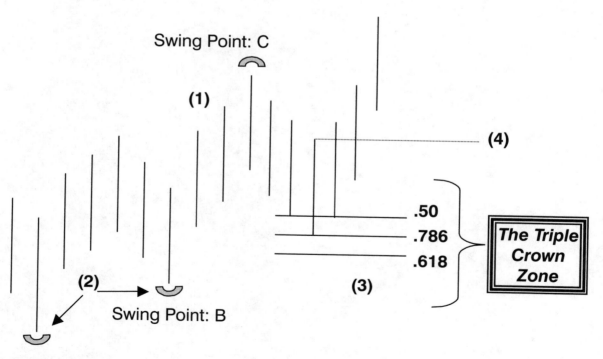

## Rules For Buys (Shorts Are Reversed)

1. A stock has formed a swing high point with a bar on each side with a lower high. Label this point C.

2. Identify the two previous low points that are below the current bar's low. Label the low point closest to point C as point "B." The swing low that is lower than B will be labeled "A."

3. There are only three Fibonacci ratios we need in this strategy. So, first calculate the .50 and .618 of low point A to high point C. At the same time, calculate the .786 retracement of low point B to high point C. To be a valid Triple Crown Zone (TCZ), the .786 retracement must fall between the .50 and .618. So, the order from the top of the zone to the bottom is .50, 785, .618.

4. If the order of the Fibonacci ratios are "valid," then we have a TCZ, and now we wait for price to come down and touch our TCZ. Once it does hit the TCZ, I look to buy above the previous bar's high.

5. Initial stops are just below the TCZ for long trades.

6. Once the swing point is made into the TCZ, which is labeled point D (because A, B, and C are the swing points used to calculate the original TCZ), we can calculate the 1.272 extension of Swing C:D. This price level serves as a trigger to initiate the trailing stop game plan.

7. When this Fibonacci price level is hit (which, by the way, means the trade is working for us), our Trailing Stop Plan takes effect:

   - Place a stop on half of the position at the higher of the previous bar low or the original entry price (breakeven).

   - On the other half, place the stop at the original entry (breakeven).

8. As a higher high is made, continue to trail the first half stop to the previous bar's low. Again, only if you make new highs do you move the stop to the previous bar's low.

9. Once the first half of the position is stopped out . . .

   - Start trailing the last half of the position at swing low points as price moves up. This allows for potential home run trades and gives room for some volatility. There is more subjectivity and discretion to this stop, but the idea is to give the trade room to breathe, but not to be foolish and turn a winner into a loser.

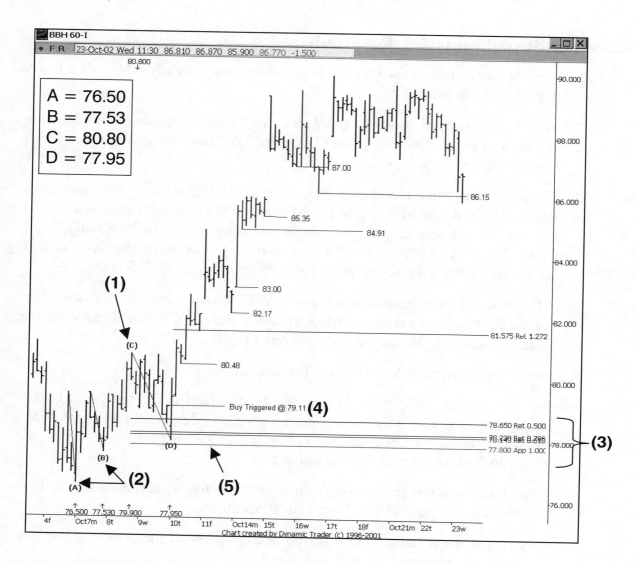

A = 76.50
B = 77.53
C = 80.80
D = 77.95

## Triple Crown Long Example:

1.  High point C is identified.

2.  Go back and label the previous two swing low points A and B.

3.  After calculating the .50 and .618 retracement of A to C and the .786 retracement of B to C, we have identified a TCZ. In fact, we also have a symmetry level at 77.80 to strengthen our TCZ.

4.  Price hits the TCZ, and I'm looking to buy above the previous bar's high. In this case, a long trade is initiated just above 79.11.

5.  The initial stop on this trade will be just below 77.80.

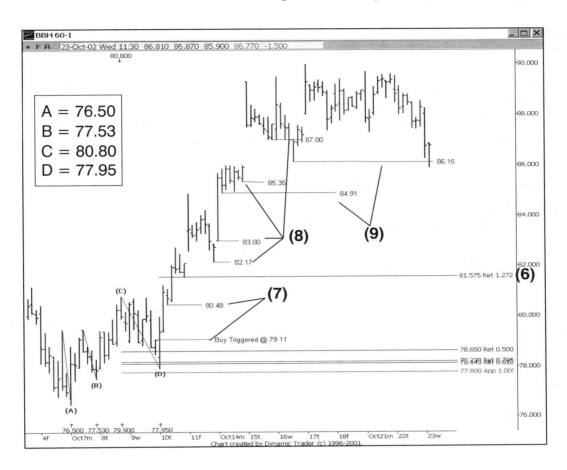

## Triple Crown Long Example:

6.  Once low point D is established and price starts to reverse up out of the TCZ, it is time to calculate the 1.272 extension of the C high to the D low. That comes in at 81.57.

7.  Trail the stop on half of the position to the previous bar's low at 80.48 after the 1.272 ratio price level is touched. The other half of the trade moves to breakeven. We are now focused on actively managing half of the position.

8.  As higher highs are made, continue trailing half of the position's stop up to the previous bar's high. This goes on for quite a few bars, and half of the trade is finally stopped out at 87.00. Over 7 points of locked-in gain. Now let's turn our focus to the stop that is sitting down at breakeven around 79.11.

9.  This final stop placement is a bit more subjective, as we want to trail it up to a previous swing low point, but still give the stock room to run. In this case, I first trail the stop up to 84.91. Price then makes a higher swing low point at 86.15 where I am ultimately stopped out of the final portion.

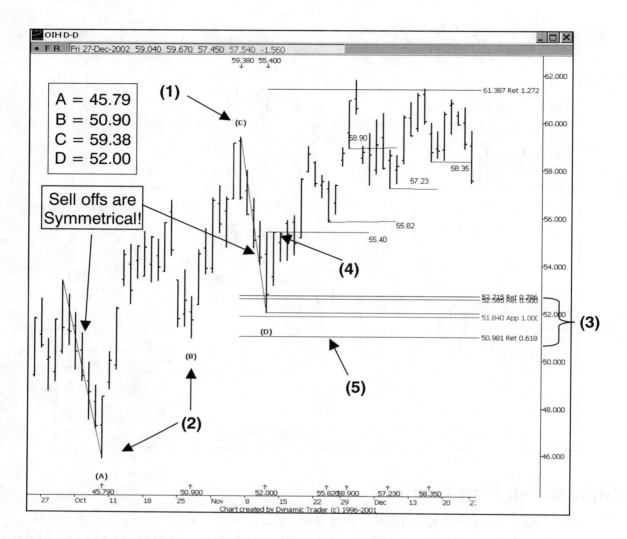

## Triple Crown Long Example:

1. High point C is identified.

2. Go back and label the previous two swing low points A and B.

3. After calculating the .50 and .618 retracement of A to C and the .786 retracement of B to C, we have identified a TCZ. The .786 is slightly above the .50, but when it is within pennies like this AND we have a symmetry level at 51.84, I will consider it a valid TCZ.

4. Price hits the TCZ, and I'm looking to buy above the previous bar's high. In this case, a long trade is initiated just above 55.40.

5. The initial stop on this trade will be just below 50.98.

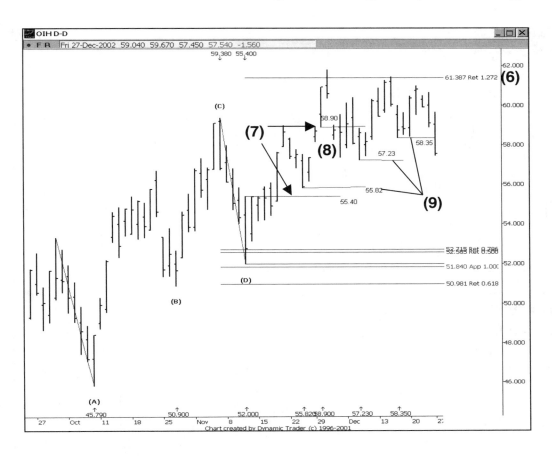

## Triple Crown Long Example:

6. Once low point D is established and price starts to reverse up out of the TCZ, it is time to calculate the 1.272 extension of the C high to the D low. That comes in at 61.38.

7. Trail the stop on half of the position to the previous bar's low at 58.90 after the 1.272 ratio price level is touched. The other half of the trade moves to breakeven. We are now focused on actively managing half of the position.

8. As soon as the 1.272 is hit, price reverses and half the position is stopped out at 58.90 for a 3.5 point profit on half. Now let's turn our focus to the stop that is sitting down at breakeven around 55.40.

9. This final stop placement is a bit more subjective, as we want to trail it up to a previous swing low point, but still give the stock room to run. In this case, I first trail the stop up to 55.82 when the first half of the trade is stopped out. Price then makes a higher swing low point at 57.23, so I move it up. Then a final higher swing low is made at 58.35, where I am ultimately stopped out of the final half of the position.

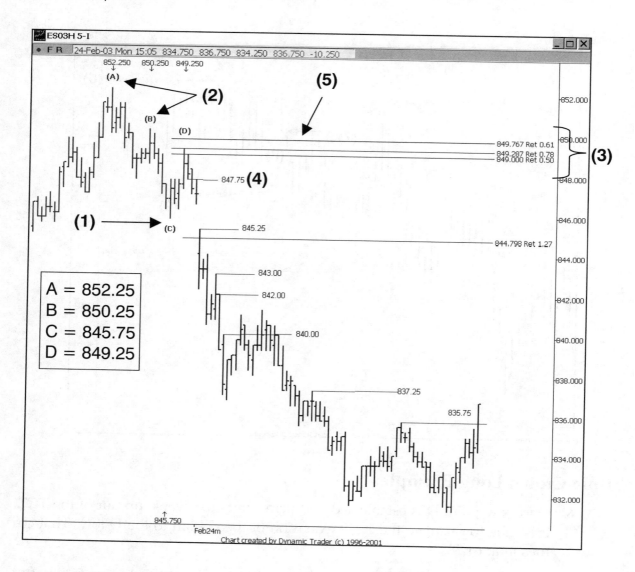

## Triple Crown Short Example:

1. Low point C is identified.

2. Go back and label the previous two swing high points A and B.

3. After calculating the .50 and .618 retracement of A to C and the .786 retracement of B to C we have identified a TCZ.

4. Price hits the TCZ, and I'm looking to short below the previous bar's low. In this case, a short trade is initiated just below 847.75 on this five-minute chart.

5. The initial stop on this trade will be just above 849.75.

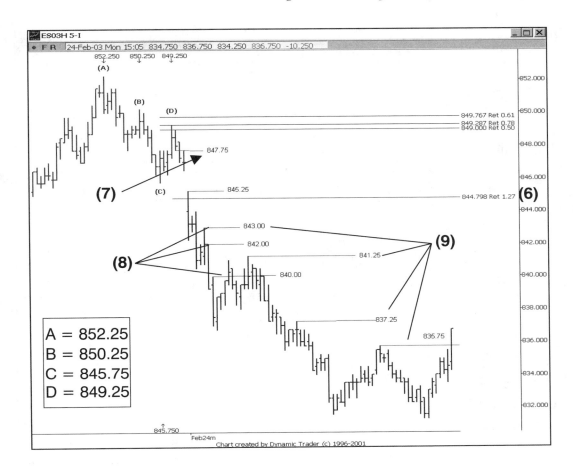

## Triple Crown Short Example:

6. Once high point D is established and price starts to reverse down out of the TCZ, it is time to calculate the 1.272 extension of the C low to the D high. That comes in at 844.75.

7. Trail the stop on half of the position to the previous bar's high. In this case, that would be the same as our entry point, so the whole position's stop is moved down to breakeven. We are now focused on actively managing half of the position as the E-mini S&P 500 futures make new lows.

8. Price continues down, and I'm able to trail half my stop as we make new lows down to 843, then to 842, then to 840, where I'm stopped out of half the position for a 7.75 point gain on a five-minute chart.

9. Now let's shift to trailing the last half of the stop down. It looks like the swing point at 843 is a good swing to use. I trail down three more times from 841.25 to 837.25, and finally to 835.75, where I'm stopped out of the last half for a 12 point profit. That's $600 per contract from a five-minute chart.

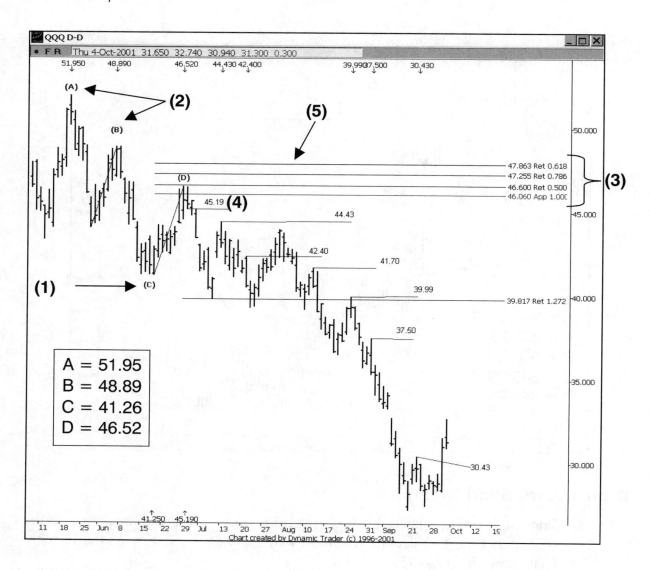

## Triple Crown Short Example:

1. Low point C is identified.

2. Go back and label the previous two swing high points A and B.

3. After calculating the .50 and .618 retracement of A to C and the .786 retracement of B to C, we have identified a TCZ with a symmetry price level at 46.06 to strengthen our zone.

4. Price hits the TCZ, and I'm looking to short below the previous bar's low. In this case, a short trade is initiated just below 45.19 on this daily chart.

5. The initial stop on this trade will be just above 47.86.

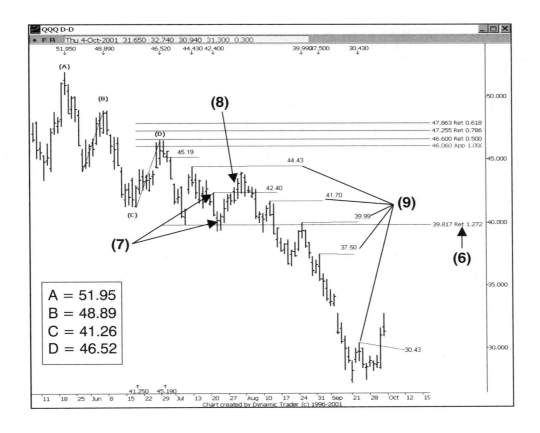

## Triple Crown Short Example:

6. Once high point D is established and price starts to reverse down out of the TCZ, it is time to calculate the 1.272 extension of the C low to the D high. That comes in at 39.81.

7. Once QQQ trades down through the 1.272 level, trail the stop on half of the position to the previous bar's high, and move the other half of the position's stop to breakeven at 45.19.

8. Unfortunately on the first half of the trade, price reverses back up against the short position, and we are stopped out at 42.40 for over 2.5 points of profit. As soon as this stop is activated, we need to focus on the other half of the position with a stop at breakeven and move it down.

9. Now let's shift to trailing the last half of the stop down. It looks like the swing point at 44.43 is a good swing to use. The stop is trailed down three additional times from 41.70 to 39.99 to 37.50 and finally to 30.43 where I'm stopped out of the last half for over 15 points of profit. The trailing stop did its job in this case and allowed us to capture a much larger profit. That's the goal—to put ourselves in the position to participate in a move like this one.

This is definitely a favorite strategy of mine. Why?

- Risk is defined and relatively tight. This translates to small losses on losing trades.

- When these trades work out, they REALLY work out! With our stop strategy, it allows these profits to run and compound.

- It is simple to calculate. You only have to look at three swing points and use three Fibonacci ratios.

- The Triple Crown identifies many different patterns and market conditions that set up for reversal. The TCZ identifies consolidating areas that are set to explode. It identifies Head and Shoulders pullbacks to the neckline, which many times yield great reversal opportunities. I have noticed that it also identifies other solid patterns like Cup & Handles, Triangles, and the list goes on. Bottom line: This specific Fibonacci price zone is very important!

Spend some time with this Zone and watch it work. You'll be pleasantly surprised.

# STRATEGY Q&A

*Question:* *How far below the TCZ do you allow price to go to still consider the zone valid?*

*Answer:* The situation where this arises most is an intraday move that slightly violates the Zone. I am a simple guy. If it looks like it has not violated the zone by too much, I would likely agree. Another requirement is that price cannot go higher than the high or lower than the low made past the TCZ. I give it one chance and one chance only. A second dip through the zone is all she wrote.

*Question:* *How did you come up with the trailing strategy?*

*Answer:* I was taking profits way too early on trades that would just make tremendous moves out of these zones. So I started holding the entire position for longer periods of time. Then I found that in choppy markets, I was losing more. So, after some hit and miss, I came up with this money management strategy that would put some money in my pocket relatively quickly and take my stop to breakeven. Then I could turn off the screens and let the charts do what they may, but at least I'm in the trade for a potential home run, and worst case (assuming no crazy gap moves), I get stopped out at breakeven.

*Question:* *If this Zone is so critical, what happens when it is broken?*

*Answer:* Great question. When a TCZ is broken, it quite often creates a momentum move in the direction in which the zone was broken.

CHAPTER **7**

# TWO-STEP PATTERNS (TSP)

# STRATEGY #4: TWO-STEP PATTERNS (TSP)

The best way to understand a TSP is to look at a picture of it. The name "two step" comes from the fact that there are two swings that move, or "step," in the same direction. The first part of the pattern is Swing A:B. The second move in this pattern is a small pullback in the opposite direction of swing A:B to point C. Then the third and final move is swing C:D, which finds price trading beyond swing point B to make a new high or low. There are three variations of this pattern that we will discuss in detail. All of these patterns create powerful trading opportunities because it is a pattern that takes advantage of "weak hands" and a "don't miss the boat" mentality exhibited by the masses.

In this chapter I first want to give a general description of the two-step pattern and how it ties into what is called the Theory of Parallel Channels. Secondly, I will describe in detail three specific types of two-step patterns (TSPs) that I use to trade with against FibZones.

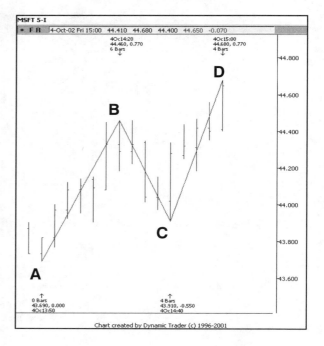

A basic two-step pattern looks like charts (1) and (2) below

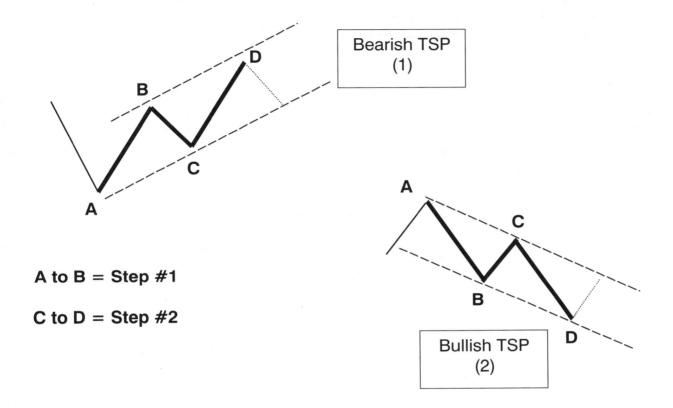

A to B = Step #1

C to D = Step #2

The concept behind a two-step pattern is that price trades within a channel in the direction of the trend. For example, in the case of a **Bearish TSP**, when price moves up from C to D and makes a new high, it is hitting a new high at the top of a channel that acts as resistance on price. So the logical place for price to trade after hitting point D is to make a similar move down like it did from B to C. The reason it is called a Bearish TSP is because we anticipate price going down from point D.

On the flipside, looking at the example of the **Bullish TSP**, the trend is down and the channel that price is trading in is down. So, when D hits the channel, it is hitting a form of support, and price is likely to trade up and retrace a percentage of the C to D move and most likely go up a similar point size of the move from B to C. What differentiates our three TSP patterns is the size of each of these steps: A to B and C to D. We will discuss these differences and characteristics in detail.

## Capture Strong Trends With The Symmetrical TSP

Now that we have defined what a two-step pattern is, we can dig into a few variations of this basic pattern. The first is called a Symmetrical TSP. We take the general two-step pattern and give definition to each step. The size of the move from A to B is equal to the size of the move from C to D. The equation is A:B = C:D.

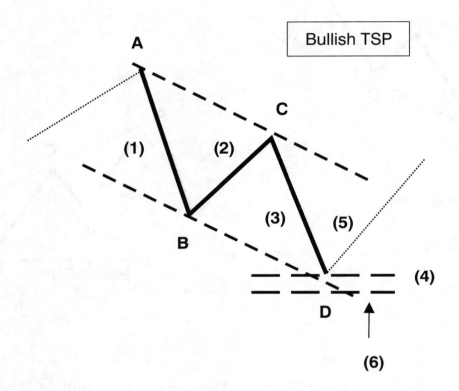

## Rules For Buys (Shorts Are Reversed)

1. A swing down is made that will be labeled A:B.

2. A pullback in the opposite direction of swing A:B is then made. This swing will be labeled B:C. Ideally, point C must not exceed the .786 retracement of swing A:B.

3. Once point C is established, price again reverses to the downside. Price must now trade below point B.

4. After low point B is violated, we will look for price to stop going down based on two items. First, a Support FibZone is calculated and defined. Second, the swing down from A to B is measured and projected from point C to determine what we will call the "Symmetry Level."

5. Once the requirements of the setup are met and price trades down to the "symmetry level" within the Support FibZone, it is "all clear" to look for opportunities to take a long trade. (See Chapter 11 for discussion on possible entry techniques.) For the example, the trigger will be a trade above the previous bar's high.

6. Initial stops on these trades will be below the Support FibZone.

7. The objective on these setups falls within the 1.272 and 1.618 extensions of swing AD.

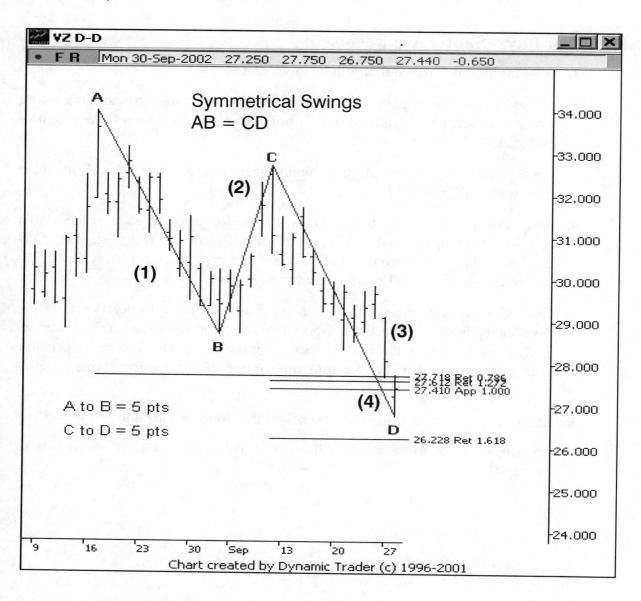

Chart created by Dynamic Trader (c) 1996-2001

## Symmetrical TSP Setup:

1. A move down from A to B.

2. Price rallies from B to C. High point C does not exceed A.

3. After establishing point C, price reverses down and goes below B.

4. The move from A to B was 5 points. From point C, we project a 5 point decline. That price level is 27.41. I call this the symmetry level.

With three other Fibonacci price levels around our symmetry level, it's time to look for an opportunity to go long and for price to reverse to the upside.

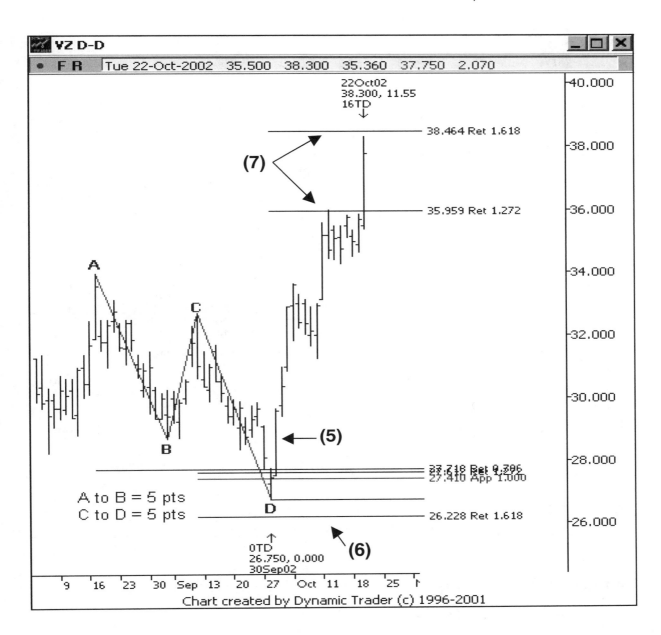

## Symmetrical TSP Result:

The result of this symmetrical two-step was quite powerful. In 16 days, Verizon (VZ) traded up almost 50%, or 11 points.

5.   The long trade was taken around $28.

6.   Initial stop was placed just below the Support FibZone around 26.20.

7.   Trade objective was between the 1.272 and 1.618 extension of swing A:D. Those prices were 35.95 to 38.46.

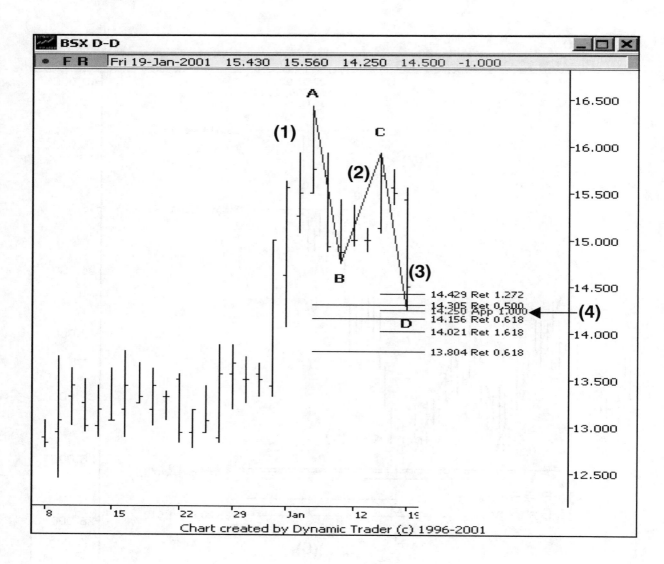

## Symmetrical TSP Setup:

1.  A move down from A to B.

2.  Price rallies from B to C. High point C does not exceed A.

3.  After establishing point C, price reverses down and goes below B.

4.  The move from A to B was about 1.6 points. From point C, we project a 1.6 point decline. That price level is 14.25. I call this the symmetry level, where C:D is symmetrical with A:B.

With five other Fibonacci price levels (Support FibZone) around our symmetry level, it's time to look for an opportunity to go long and for price to reverse to the upside.

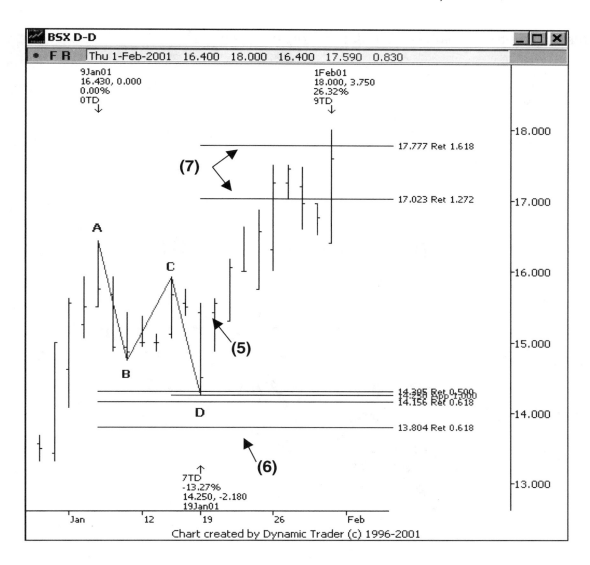

## Symmetrical TSP Result:

The result of this symmetrical two step was also quite powerful. Notice the day after point D is formed, Boston Scientific jumps higher at the open, and in 9 days, BSX traded up over 26% or 3.75 points.

5. A long trade was taken around $15.50.

6. Initial stop was placed just below the Support FibZone around 13.70.

7. Trade objective was between the 1.272 and 1.618 extension of swing A:D. Those prices were 17.02 to 17.77.

Let's reverse the scenario and look for short trade setups.

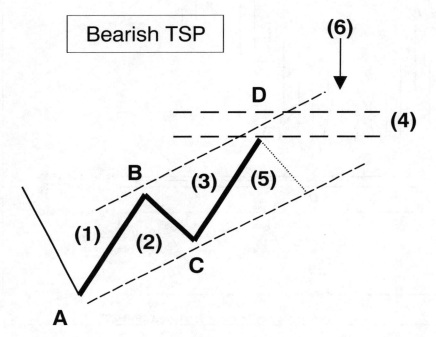

## Rules For a Bearish TSP (Shorts):

1. A swing up is made that will be labeled A:B.

2. A pullback in the opposite direction of swing A:B is then made. This swing will be labeled B:C. Point C ideally will not exceed the .786 retracement of swing A:B. The only requirement is that C does not trade below point A.

3. Once point C is established, price again reverses to the upside. Price must now trade above point B.

4. After high point B is violated to the upside, we will look for price to rally, but find resistance higher based on two items. First, a Resistance FibZone is calculated and defined. Second, the swing up from A to B is measured and projected from point C to determine what we will call the "Symmetry Level."

5. Once the requirements of the setup are met and price trades up to the "symmetry level" within the Resistance FibZone, it is clear to look for opportunities to take a short trade.

6. Initial stops on these trades will be above the Resistance FibZone.

7. The objective on these setups falls within the 1.272 and 1.618 extensions of swing A:D.

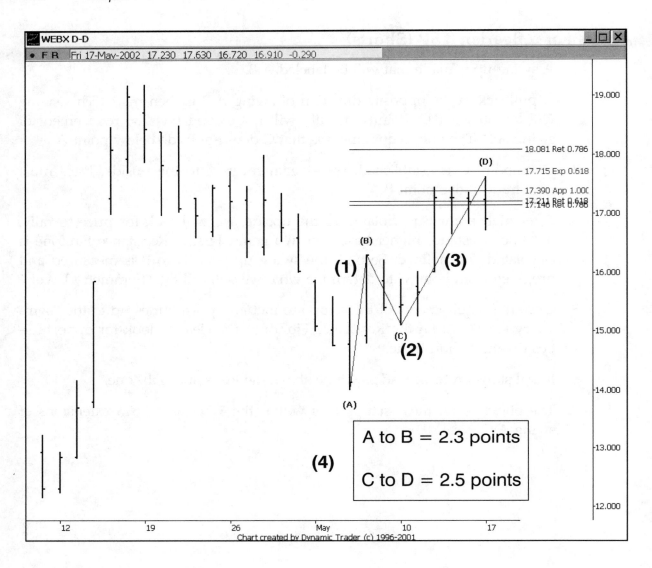

Chart created by Dynamic Trader (c) 1996-2001

## Bearish Symmetrical TSP Setup:

1. A move up from A to B.

2. Price falls from B to C. Low point C does not exceed A.

3. After establishing point C, price reverses up and goes above B.

4. The move from A to B was 2.3 points. From point C, we project a 2.3 point rally. That price level is 17.39. I call this the symmetry level.

With four other Fibonacci price levels around our symmetry level, it's time to look for an opportunity to go short and for price to reverse to the downside.

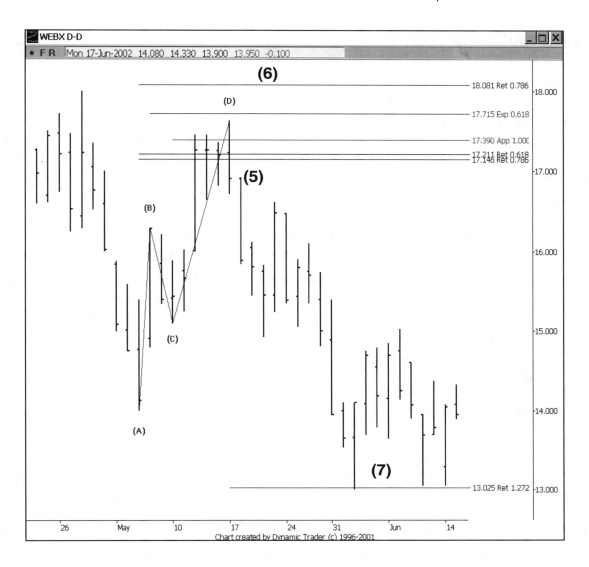

## Bearish Symmetrical TSP Result:

After Webex tested our FibZone for a few days, it sold off over 4.5 points and immediately went down to the 1.272 extension of swing A:D.

5.  A short trade was taken around $16.50.

6.  Initial stop was placed just above the Resistance FibZone around 18.10.

7.  Trade objective was between the 1.272 and 1.618 extension of swing A:D. Webex formed a double bottom against the 1.272 extension at 13.02, which would be a warning sign to consider taking profits.

# STRATEGY Q&A

**Question:** *Do you ever take profits before the 1.272 or 1.618 retracement?*

**Answer:** Yes. Many times I have found a resistance or Support FibZone that stands between my entry and the ultimate 1.272 to 1.618 objective. If this FibZone is of significant size (number of price levels), then I will consider taking a portion of my trade off at that intermediate level and trailing my stop. This is especially beneficial in markets that are not trending and very choppy. When a stock is in a strong trend, I typically do not have to do this.

**Question:** *Sometimes the number of bars from A to B are significantly more or less than the C to D swing, but the swings are still symmetrical in price. Does this matter?*

**Answer:** Generally speaking, the number of bars to complete each step are not critical. Sometimes the two-step pattern does not look all that pretty, but the concept we are trying to capitalize on is the fact that each of these swings are equal in price. Of course, the pattern does have to pass the basic visual test. So, if you look at a chart and the move from A to B is 5 bars and the move from C to D is 40 bars, I would not classify it as a two-step pattern. Use common sense here.

**Question:** *Is this considered a reversal or is it momentum trading with this pattern?*

**Answer:** The answer to this question—for this pattern and ALL patterns in this book—is based on the size of the pattern. For example, we may be looking at a symmetrical two-step pattern where A to B is 20 points and C to D is 20 points, leaving current price at, say, 15. This would be considered a reversal setup. However, if we are in a major up trend and the price of the stock is $50 and the A to B and C to D steps down are each only 1 point, then this would be considered a micro-pattern pullback setting up for a continuation/momentum trade. It is all based on the size of the pattern to determine whether it's a reversal or momentum trade. These setups occur on all time frames and in many sizes.

## Enter Pullbacks Using The Gartley TSP

We have just looked at one variation of a Two-Step Pattern (TSP). Now let's look at the second of three, called a Gartley. Forty-year trading veteran Larry Pesavento published this pattern in his book *Fibonacci Ratios with Pattern Recognition* (1997). Larry originally saw the outline of this pattern in H. M. Gartley's 1932 book *Profits In The Stock Market*. No Fibonacci ratios were assigned to the pattern in this book. It was Larry who ultimately added Fibonacci to the Gartley price structure. In the context of his trading, Larry stated that the Gartley is "one of the best patterns I ever found." I agree.

For purposes of this book, I have titled the pattern a "Gartley TSP" because within this pattern is an A:B = C:D two-step pattern (TSP). Specific Fibonacci ratios apply to this pattern, so let's look at the setup for a Bullish Gartley TSP.

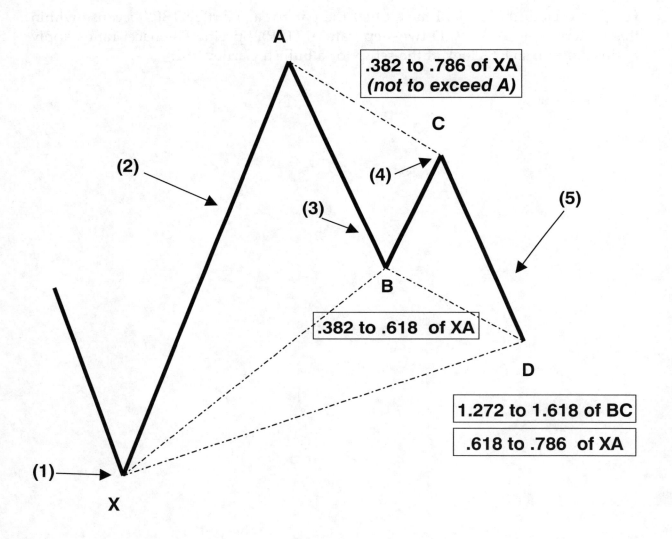

Bullish Gartley TSP

A

.382 to .786 of XA
*(not to exceed A)*

C

(2)

(4)

(3)

(5)

B

.382 to .618 of XA

D

1.272 to 1.618 of BC

.618 to .786 of XA

(1)

X

## Rules For Buys: (Shorts Are Reversed):

1. A low point, "X", is determined on the chart. X will be the lowest low in this entire pattern. If price falls below X, the Bullish Gartley TSP will be void.

2. From point X, a rally occurs up to a swing high point we will label A. This swing high is the highest high in the entire pattern. If price goes above A before pattern completion, the Bullish Gartley TSP will be invalid.

3. Now that the upper and lower swing points of the pattern are established, we are looking for a move down from point A to the low point labeled B. This will be labeled Swing A:B. B should be between the .382 and .618 retracement of swing X:A.

4. A pullback in the opposite direction of swing A:B is then made up to point C. This swing will be labeled B:C. Point C ideally falls between the .382 and .786 retracement of swing A:B. The only hard requirement is that point C does not exceed point A.

5. Once point C is established, price again reverses to the downside. Price must now trade below point B and down between the .618 to .786 retracement of Swing X:A. Once price reaches this level, a Bullish Gartley TSP has been completed, and we look for opportunities to buy.

6. In this case, we will enter above the previous day's high.

7. The initial stop will be below the Support FibZone.

8. The first objective is at the first major Resistance FibZone

9. The final objective is the 1.272 extension of swing A:D.

The key differences between the Bullish Gartley TSP and the Bullish Symmetrical TSP are:

- An additional reference low point "X" is added into the mix. We gauge points B and D from this point with Fibonacci ratios. Low point B should be between the .382 and .50 retracement of swing X:A. Low point D should be between the .618 and .786 retracement of swing X:A. Point D is even stronger when it is also the 1.272 or 1.618 extension of swing B:C.

- The step from A to B does not necessarily have to "equal" C to D. A to B may be longer or shorter in size than the C to D move. That is fine because this pattern is not defined by symmetry, but by specific Fibonacci ratios.

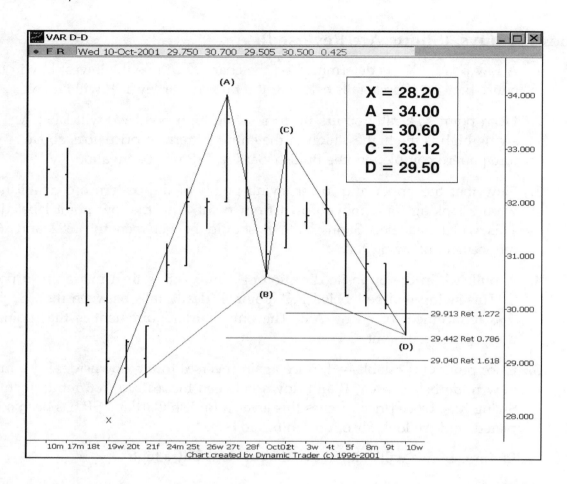

## Bullish Gartley TSP Setup:

1.  Low point X is determined.

2.  A rally occurs and establishes high point A. X and A now serve as the boundaries of the pattern.

3.  Price falls to B, which turns out to be between the .50 and .618 retracement of swing X:A. This is a valid swing point, so the pattern is currently valid.

4.  VAR rallies up to the .786 retracement of swing A:B. It does not violate the high at A, so at this point, we are 1 point away from a complete setup.

5.  Price, in fact, reverses down to D and makes a low point at the .786 of Swing X:A and between the 1.272 and 1.618 extension of swing B:C.

Our pattern is valid at this point, so it's time to look for a long trade. (See Chapter 11 for possible entry techniques.)

VAR D-D

F R Tue 27-Nov-2001 37.360 38.250 35.950 35.950 -1.405

X = 28.20
A = 34.00
B = 30.60
C = 33.12
D = 29.50

36.786 Ret 1.618
35.229 Ret 1.272
(9)
(8)
(A)
(C)
32.258 Ret 0.786
32.030 App 1.000
31.753 Ret 0.508
(6)
(B)
29.913 Ret 1.272
(D)
29.442 Ret 0.786
29.040 Ret 1.618
(7)
X

'21   '28   Oct   '12   '19   '26   Nov   '9   '16   '23

Chart created by Dynamic Trader (c) 1996-2001

## Bullish Gartley TSP Result:

After VAR completed the pattern, the stock rallies over 8 points!

6. A simple trigger to use to enter these patterns is a trade above the previous day's high. In this case, I entered at 30.71.

7. Initial stop was placed just below the Support FibZone around 29.00.

8. I take profits in two stages. The first stage is when price meets the first Resistance FibZone that includes the symmetry level of swing B:C. In this case, that Resistance FibZone was from 31.75–32.25. My rule is to take profits on half when price trades below the previous day's low after touching the price zone. In this case, it was 31.99. At this point, I also move my stop to breakeven.

9. My final objective on the trade is between the 1.272 and 1.618 extension of swing A:D. I take profits on the rest of the position on a trade below the previous bar's low after touching the 1.272 extension of swing A:D. That was at 35.25.

Let's reverse the scenario and look for setups for short trades.

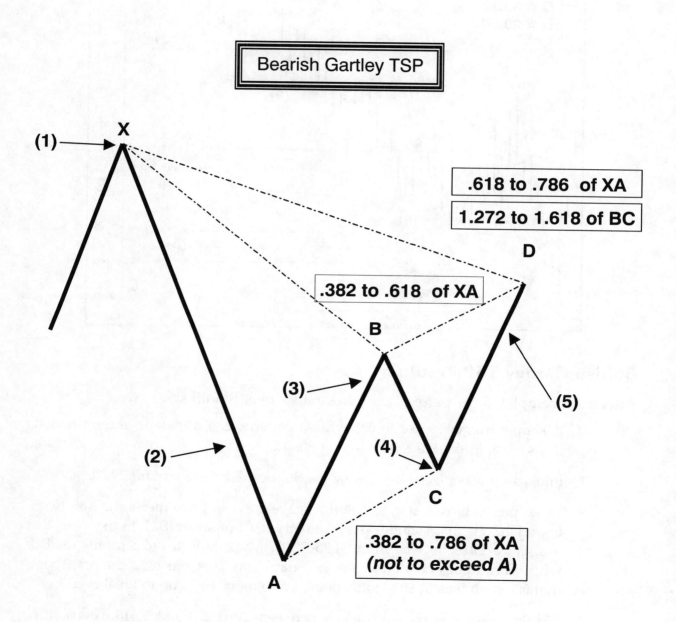

Bearish Gartley TSP

.618 to .786 of XA

1.272 to 1.618 of BC

.382 to .618 of XA

.382 to .786 of XA
(*not to exceed A*)

## Rules For Shorts (Buys Are Reversed):

1. A high point, "X", is determined on the chart. X will be the highest high in this entire pattern. If price rallies above X, the Bearish Gartley TSP will be void.

2. From point X, a selloff occurs down to a swing low point we will label point A. This swing low is the lowest low in the entire pattern. If price goes below A before pattern completion, the Bearish Gartley TSP will be void.

3. Now that the upper and lower swing points of the pattern are established, we are looking for a move up from point A to a swing high point labeled B.

4. A pullback in the opposite direction of swing A:B is then made. This swing will be labeled B:C. Point C must not exceed the .786 retracement of swing A:B. It does not need to go all the way to .786, but should at least go to the .382 retracement of swing A:B.

5. Once point C is established, price again reverses to the upside. Price must now trade above point B and up to the .618 to .786 retracement of Swing X:A. Once price reaches this level, a Bearish Gartley TSP has been completed, and we look for opportunities to sell short.

6. In this case, we will enter below the previous day's low.

7. The initial stop will be below the Support FibZone.

8. The first objective is at the first major Support FibZone

9. The final objective is the 1.272 extension of swing A:D.

The key differences between the Bearish Gartley TSP and the Bearish Symmetrical TSP are:

1. An additional reference high point, "X", is added into the mix. We gauge points B and D from this point with Fibonacci ratios. High point B should be between the .382 and .50 retracement of swing X:A. High point D should be between the .618 and .786 retracement of swing X:A. Point D is even stronger when it is also the 1.272 or 1.618 extension of swing B:C.

2. The step from A to B does not necessarily have to "equal" C to D. A to B may be longer or shorter in size than the C to D move. That is fine because this pattern is not defined by symmetry, but by specific Fibonacci ratios.

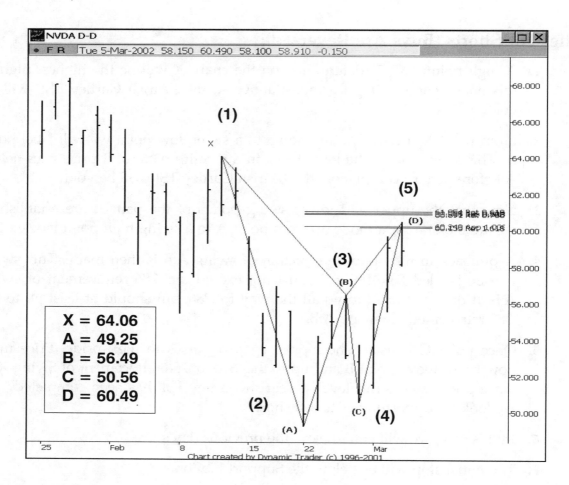

**Bearish Gartley TSP Setup:**

1.  High point X is determined.

2.  A selloff occurs and establishes low point A. X and A now serve as the boundaries of the pattern.

3.  Price rallies to B, which turns out to be between the .50 retracement of swing X:A. This is a valid swing point, so the pattern is currently valid.

4.  NVDA reverses down to the .786 retracement of swing A:B. It does not violate the low at A, so at this point, we are one point away from a complete setup.

5.  Price, in fact, reverses up and rallies to D and makes a high point at the .786 of Swing X:A and between the 1.272 and 1.618 extension of swing B:C.

Our pattern is valid at this point, so it's time to look for a short trade against the Resistance FibZone where the pattern has completed.

## Bearish Gartley TSP Result:

After NVDA completed the pattern, the stock declines over 20 points!

6.  A simple trigger to use to enter these patterns is a trade below the previous day's low. In this case, I entered around 57.15.

7.  The initial stop will be above the Resistance FibZone around 62.00.

8.  I take profits in two stages. The first stage is when price meets the first Support FibZone that includes the symmetry level of swing B:C. In this case, that Resistance FibZone was from 53.54–54.87. My rule is to take profits on half when price trades above the previous day's high after touching the price zone. In this case, it was 52.83. At this point, I also move my stop to breakeven.

9.  My final objective on the trade is between the 1.272 and 1.618 extension of swing A:D. I take profits on the rest of the position on a trade above the previous bar's high after touching the 1.272 extension of swing A:D. That was at 49.55. Note that NVDA falls another 9 points after I'm out!

X = 822.25
A = 836.75
B = 829.75
C = 835.75
D = 828.00

## Intraday Gartley TSP Setup:

1. Low point X is determined on this five-minute chart.

2. A rally occurs and establishes high point A. X and A now serve as the boundaries of the pattern.

3. Price falls to point B, which turns out to be between the .50 retracement of swing X:A. This is a valid swing point, so the pattern is currently valid.

4. ES03H rallies up to the .786 retracement of swing A:B. It does not violate the high at A, so at this point we are one point away from a complete setup.

5. Price, in fact, reverses down to D and makes a low point at the .786 of swing X:A and between the 1.272 and 1.618 extension of swing B:C.

Our pattern is valid at this point, so it's time to look for a long trade.

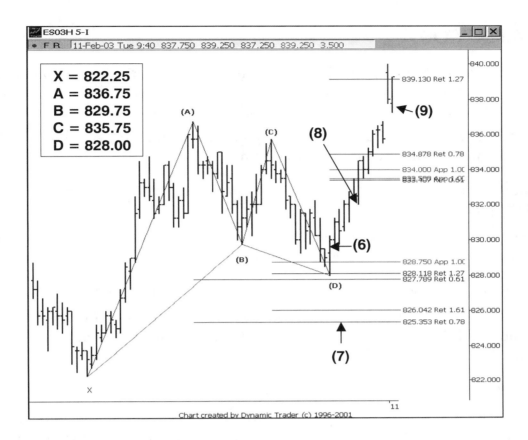

ESO3H 5-I

F R 11-Feb-03 Tue 9:40 837.750 839.250 837.250 839.250 3.500

X = 822.25
A = 836.75
B = 829.75
C = 835.75
D = 828.00

839.130 Ret 1.27
(9)
(8)
834.878 Ret 0.78
834.000 App 1.00
833.589 Ret 0.61
(6)
828.750 App 1.00
828.118 Ret 1.27
827.789 Ret 0.61
826.042 Ret 1.61
825.353 Ret 0.78
(7)

Chart created by Dynamic Trader (c) 1996-2001

## Intraday Gartley TSP Result:

*After ESO3H completed the pattern, the contract rallied over 11 points!*

6. A simple trigger to use to enter these patterns is a trade above the previous day's high after price completes the pattern. In this case, I entered around 829.50.

7. Initial stop was placed just below the Support FibZone around 825.00.

8. I take profits in two stages. The first stage is when price meets the first Support FibZone that includes the symmetry level of swing B:C. In this case, that Resistance FibZone was from 833.25–835.00. My rule is to take profits on half when price trades below the previous day's low after touching this price zone. In this case, it was 832.50. At this point, I also move my stop to breakeven.

9. My final objective on the trade is between the 1.272 and 1.618 extension of swing A:D. I take profits on the rest of the position on trade below the previous low after touching the 1.272 extension of swing A:D. That was at 837.75. Not bad for a five-minute chart.

# STRATEGY Q&A

*Question:* *You mention an easy trigger to use for longs is a trade above the previous day's high after completing the pattern and for shorts when price trades below the previous day's low after pattern completion. Do you use different triggers?*

*Answer:* Yes. We will discuss in later chapters the various triggers that I will consider and on what time frame I look for them.

*Question:* *Do you need a FibZone around the pattern completion level before you will consider taking the trade?*

*Answer:* Yes. I want a total of at least three Fibonacci price levels acting as support or resistance before I will consider the trade.

*Question:* *Should someone trading this pattern use your stop loss rules?*

*Answer:* I believe you have to "own" whatever you do. If this stop loss strategy that I have outlined fits your style . . . go for it! However, if it doesn't fit, find a stop loss program that does fit.

*Question:* *What time frames work best for these patterns?*

*Answer:* I've traded these patterns all the way down to five-minute charts, and they work just as accurately as do the daily or weekly charts. The highest time frame I have traded these patterns on were monthly charts. I tend to trade the daily and weekly patterns more than any other. The time frame chosen will be largely dependent upon how much risk your money management plan allows you to take per trade (to be discussed later). Remember, the Gartley is "officially complete" when it reaches the .618 retracement of swing X:A. However, it can go down to the .786 retracement of X:A and still be valid. The higher the time frame you go, and the bigger the pattern, the bigger the gap between the .618 and .786, which translates to a larger point risk if a trade is initiated at the .618 level. Sometimes by waiting on a trigger to enter, it keeps a trader patient until price goes deeper into the FibZone between the .618 and .786 before being called to take the trade leaving less point risk.

## Find Powerful Reversals With The Butterfly TSP

The "Butterfly Pattern" is a TSP-type pattern that was discovered by Bryce Gilmore and Larry Pesavento. This pattern allows you to find significant bottom and top turning points in the markets. The Butterfly is a "hybrid" of the Gartley. The key difference in this pattern vs. the Gartley is the fact that point D completes between the 1.272 and 1.618 extension of X:A vs. the .618 to .786 for a Gartley. It can be traded as a large reversal pattern, or if spotted on a smaller/micro time frame within the context of a larger trend, it could be used for momentum/continuation trading. Why the name? When you look at this pattern with the specific ratios attached to each swing and connect the dots, the pattern looks just like a butterfly in flight.

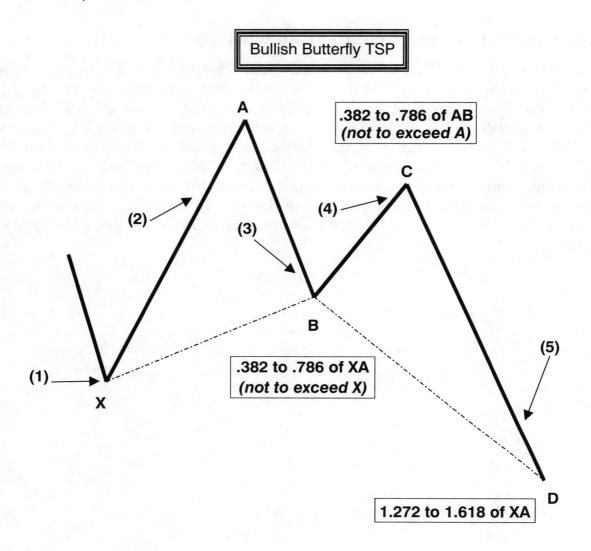

**Bullish Butterfly TSP**

.382 to .786 of AB
*(not to exceed A)*

.382 to .786 of XA
*(not to exceed X)*

1.272 to 1.618 of XA

## Rules For Buys (Shorts Are Reversed):

1. Point X—The beginning point of the pattern and the second lowest point in the entire pattern. It will be the "anchor" point to calculate the pattern completion level at point D.

2. Point A—The highest high of the pattern.

3. Point B—This will ideally fall between the .382 and .786 retracement of Swing X:A. The only hard rule here is that point B cannot fall below point X.

4. Point C—The only hard requirement for this point is that it be lower than point A. Ideally, it hits one of our retracement levels at .382, .50, .618, or .786 of swing A:B.

5. Point D—This is the critical point. Once point C is established and price falls and trades below point B, we calculate the 1.272 and 1.618 extension of swing X:A. This will provide the pattern completion zone. Point D must be lower than point X.

At this point, if you "connect the dots" in the following order . . .

X to A

X to B

A to B

B to C

B to D

C to D

. . . you should be able to see the outline of what looks like a butterfly. Sometimes the butterfly is a little distorted depending on the time between swing points, but it should look like a Butterfly with its right wing dipping down lower than the left. Let's look at a couple of examples.

6. For illustration purposes, we will enter a long trade above the previous day's high. (See Chapter 11 for other trigger ideas.)

7. Initial stop on the trade is below the Support FibZone.

8. The first objective will be between the .618 and .786 retracement of swing C:D.

9. The final objective is the 1.272 extension of swing A:D.

The key differences between the Bullish Butterfly TSP and the Bullish Gartley TSP are:

1. Point B can go lower in the Butterfly TSP vs. the Gartley TSP.

2. Point D goes below X and, by definition, falls between the 1.272 to 1.618 extension of swing X:A. The Gartley TSP has D completing within the X:A swing between the .618 and .786 retracement of X:A.

3. The step from A to B does not necessarily have to "equal" C to D. C to D is typically longer than A:B. There are situations where A:B does equal C:D, which means we could have a Symmetrical TSP AND a Butterfly TSP all rolled into one.

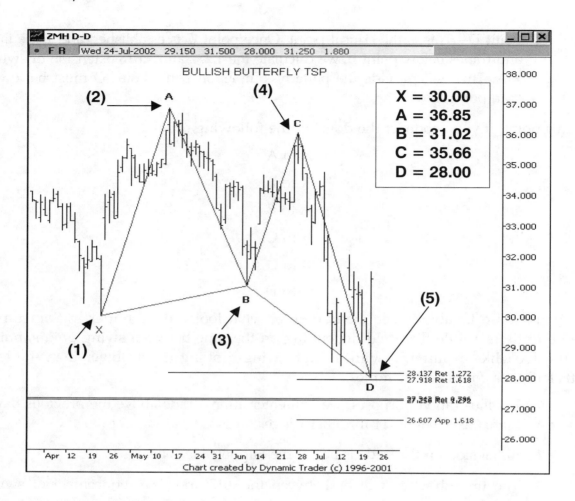

BULLISH BUTTERFLY TSP

| X = 30.00 |
| A = 36.85 |
| B = 31.02 |
| C = 35.66 |
| D = 28.00 |

28.137 Ret 1.272
27.918 Ret 1.618
27.368 Ret 1.796
26.607 App 1.618

Chart created by Dynamic Trader (c) 1996-2001

## Bullish Butterfly TSP Setup:

1. A low point, X, is made in April at 30.00.

2. Price rallies to point A and forms a swing high at 36.85. This is the highest high in the pattern.

3. Low point B is made at 31.02 around the .786 retracement of X:A. Remember, the only hard requirement here is that we don't go below X.

4. A 6 point rally unfolds and high point C is made at 35.66 around the .786 retracement of A:B. Here, the only requirement is that we don't exceed point A.

5. Over the course of the next four weeks, ZMH sells off 8 points and hits a Support FibZone from 26.60–28.13. On July 24, ZMH hits the 1.272 extension of X:A to officially complete our pattern. Now we look for opportunities to go long. (See Chapter 11 on Triggers for potential ideas on how to look for entry opportunities once a pattern completes.)

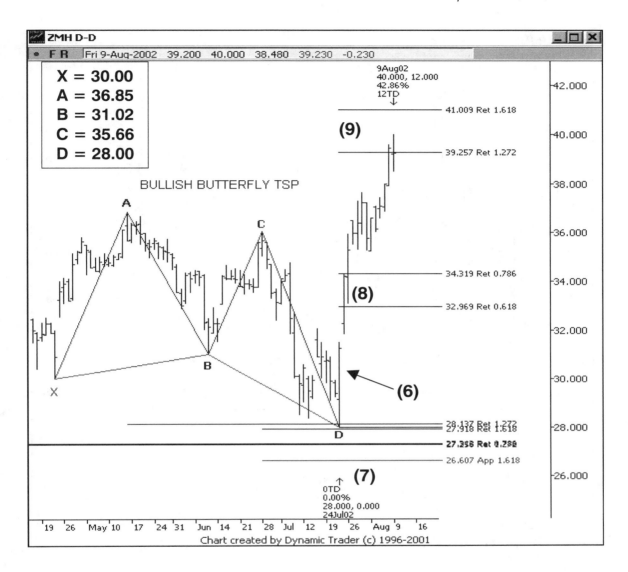

## Bullish Butterfly TSP Result:

This pattern resulted in a 42% rally from point D, or roughly 12 points of possible profits, in 12 trading sessions.

6. The same day ZMH hits our Support FibZone, we go long.

7. The initial stop is just below the FibZone around 26.60.

8. First profits are taken at the .618 to .786 retracement of swing C:D.

9. The final objective on these trades is around the 1.272 to 1.618 extension of swing A:D.

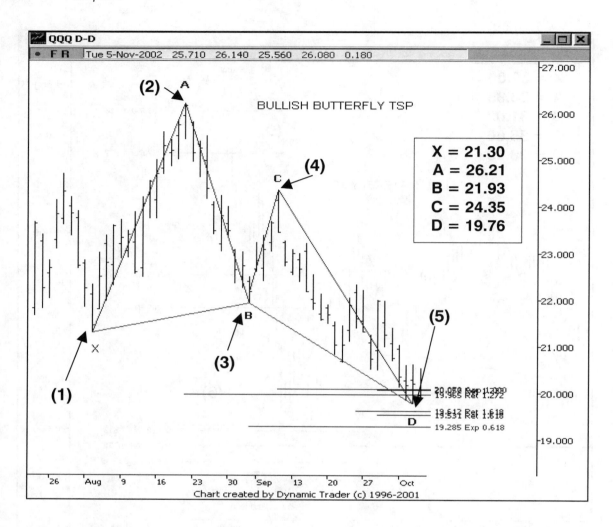

## Bullish Butterfly TSP Setup:

1.  A low point, X, is made in August at 21.30.

2.  Price rallies to point A and forms a swing high point at 26.21. This is the highest high in the pattern.

3.  Low point B is made at 21.93 around the .786 retracement of X:A. Remember, the only hard requirement here is that we don't go below X.

4.  A small rally unfolds and high point C is made at 24.35 around the .50 retracement of A:B. Here, the only requirement is that we don't exceed point A.

5.  Over the course of the next four weeks, QQQ sells off 4 points and hits a Support FibZone from 19.28–20.05. QQQ hits the 1.272 extension of X:A to officially complete our pattern at 19.96.

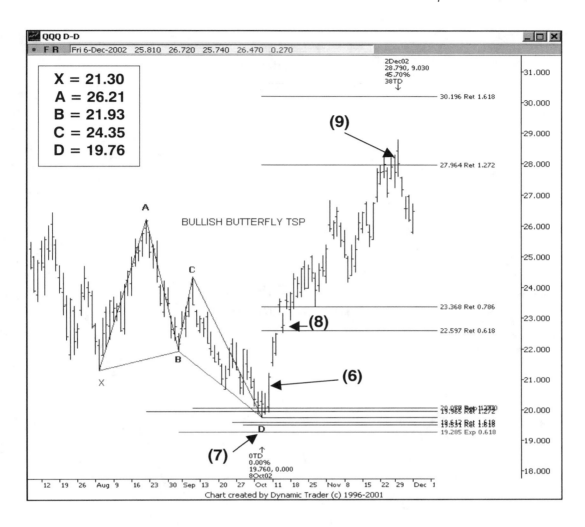

Chart created by Dynamic Trader (c) 1996-2001

## Bullish Butterfly TSP Result:

In a little over one month, QQQ rose over 45%, or 9 points.

6. A long trade is entered around 20.50 above the previous day's high after pattern completion.

7. The initial stop loss is just below 19.25.

8. As soon as a swing point D is established, I immediately calculate Fibonacci price resistance levels that will tell me where price will face major decisions. The first level that I look to take profits is between the .618 and .786 retracement of C:D. At this level, I typically take half the position off and move my stop up to reduce or eliminate risk.

9. The final objective on these trades is around the 1.272 to 1.618 extension of swing A:D. In this situation, we took profits between 27.00 and 28.00.

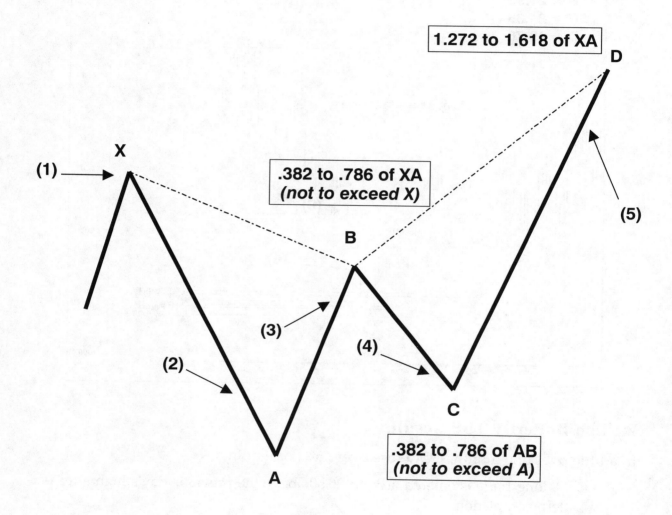

Bearish Butterfly TSP

1.272 to 1.618 of XA

.382 to .786 of XA
*(not to exceed X)*

.382 to .786 of AB
*(not to exceed A)*

## Rules For Short Sales (Buys Are Reversed):

1. Point X—The beginning point of the pattern is the second highest point in the entire pattern. It will be the "anchor" point to calculate the pattern completion level at point D.

2. Point A—The lowest low of the pattern.

3. Point B—This is typically between a .382 and .786 retracement of Swing X:A.

4. Point C—The only hard requirement for this point is that it be higher than point A. Ideally, it hits one of our retracement levels at .50, .618, or .786 of Swing A:B.

5. Point D—This is the critical point. Once point C is established and price rallies and trades above point B, we calculate the 1.272 and 1.618 extension of swing X:A. This will provide the pattern-completion level. Point D must be higher than point X.

At this point, if you "connect the dots" in the following order . . .

X to A

X to B

A to B

B to C

B to D

C to D

. . . you should be able to see the outline of what looks like a butterfly. Sometimes the butterfly is a little distorted depending on the time between swing points, but it should look like a Butterfly with its right wing pushing higher than the left. Let's look at a couple of examples.

6. For illustration purposes, we will enter a short trade below the previous day's low. (See Chapter 11 for other trigger ideas.)

7. Initial stop on the trade is above the Resistance FibZone.

8. The first objective will be between the .618 and .786 retracement of swing C:D.

9. The final objective is between the 1.272 and 1.618 extension of swing A:D.

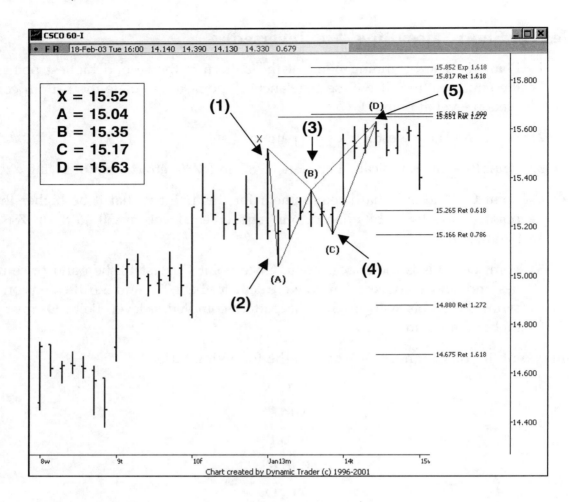

X = 15.52
A = 15.04
B = 15.35
C = 15.17
D = 15.63

## Bearish Butterfly TSP Setup:

1.  A high point, X, is made 15.52 on this 60-minute chart.

2.  Price declines to point A and forms a swing low point at 15.04. This is the lowest low in the pattern.

3.  High point B is made at 15.35 around the .50 retracement of X:A. Remember, the only hard requirement here is that price cannot go above point X.

4.  A small decline unfolds and low point C is made at 15.17 around the .50 retracement of A:B. Here, the only requirement is that we don't trade below point A.

5.  CSCO rallies from point C and hits a Resistance FibZone from 15.60–15.85 that includes the 1.272 extension of X:A to officially complete our pattern. Now we look for opportunities to go short. (See Chapter 11 on Triggers for potential ideas on how to look for entry opportunities once a pattern completes.)

## Bearish Butterfly TSP Result:

From this pattern on a 60-minute chart, CSCO falls over 1.6 points in three days.

6. A short is entered around 15.50.

7. The initial stop loss is just above 15.85.

8. As soon as swing point D is established, I immediately calculate Fibonacci price support levels that will tell me where price will face major decisions. The first level that I look to take profits is between the .618 and .786 retracement of C:D. At this level, I typically take half the position off and move my stop up to reduce or eliminate risk. In the situation above, you may decide to simply tighten stops due to the minimal amount of movement it took to get to these levels.

9. The final objective on these trades is around the 1.272 to 1.618 extension of swing A:D. Once this zone is hit, I occasionally use the previous bar's high as a trailing stop as price makes lower lows to see if we can maximize and ride out a larger winner.

**Let's drill down to a daily chart to look at price action . . .** →

23Mar02
75 Wk
↓

DOWN 20 PTS!

18 Wk
-20.220
27Jul02

WMT W-W

• F R    Sat 9-Nov-2002    54.560    54.770    53.200    53.450    -1.100

Chart created by Dynamic Trader (c) 1996-2001

You're probably thinking, *"Wait a minute here. This chart doesn't have a Bearish Butterfly TSP setup."* You're right, but over this two-year time frame, how would you have known that the high made during the week of March 23, 2002, was going to lead to a 20 point selloff in Wal-Mart (WMT)? On the next page, check out what was forming at this weekly chart peak when we drilled down to the daily chart.

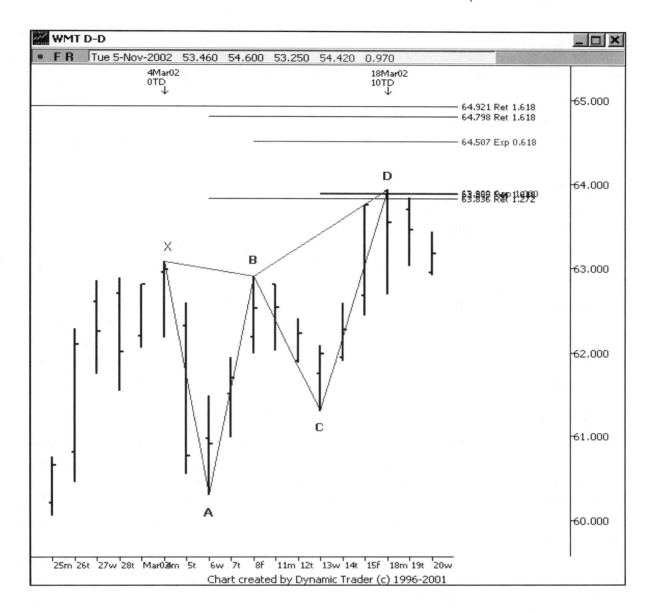

When we drill down to the daily chart of Wal-Mart (WMT) and look closer, we see that our Bearish Butterfly TSP pattern developed against a Resistance FibZone. Point D of this pattern was THE high in 2002. This pattern is often found at significant high and low points. In this case, it led to a 20 point selloff (as seen from the previous page).

# STRATEGY Q&A

*Question: Do you enter the trade as soon as the pattern completes at point D?*

*Answer:* Personally, I do not enter right when the pattern hits the 1.272 extension. I almost always look for a trigger to enter. When trading this pattern on a daily time frame or higher, this pattern is usually occurring in the midst of a strong trend, which means I would be going against the grain. That's fine, but I don't want to be stepping in front of oncoming traffic either. So, I look for a trigger.

For example, let's say a Bullish Butterfly TSP is official as price hits the 1.272 extension of swing X:A. A simple trigger would be to only take a long trade if price goes above the previous day's high. That previous day's high acts as the "trigger" for me to take action and go long. That is a simple trigger. More complex triggers are discussed later in this book. That being said, I know many people that successfully trade these patterns that enter the trade as soon as price hits the 1.272 Fibonacci extension level with the thought process that there is less risk. I agree that there is potentially less "point risk," but there is no structural price confirmation that price is reversing, so there is a higher likelihood of getting stopped out in my opinion. Regardless of how you chose to enter into these trades, stops must be used.

*Question: I see that you take profits in two stages. Why is this?*

*Answer:* This is risk control for me. I'm not trying to hit home runs. I want to position myself to benefit from a home run trade, but I realize most trades are going to be base hits. So, I take half profits at the "base hit level" and trail my stop to a closer level (*ideally at breakeven, if the chart allows*). If price keeps moving in my favor, then great . . . I'll benefit. If not, that's fine, because I've locked in profits and I'll get stopped out with little or no damage on the last half of the trade. There are many ways to take profits and trail stops. I have found this strategy to work best for me. The key concept to remember is to lock in profits on a portion of the trade as soon as possible and let the rest of the trade move as it may with a focus on reducing and eliminating risk by trailing the stop order as a trade moves in your favor.

CHAPTER **8**

# HEISENBERG 200

# STRATEGY #5: HEISENBERG 200

The 200-day Simple Moving Average (SMA) is a highly watched level by institutional investors, and Wall Street research outfits. In the case of the 200-day SMA, there is a mass belief and following that one should be a buyer when price crosses above the 200-day SMA and a seller when it crosses below. I don't know how many times I've turned on the TV to watch my financial soap operas and hear that a "Street firm" has upgraded XYZ Corp. for reasons supposedly related to an improving fundamental outlook. So when I pull up a chart of that company, where is price sitting? Lo and behold, it's sitting on the 200-day SMA. Countless timing systems have been constructed around the 200-day SMA following the same concept to be a buyer above the 200-day SMA and a seller below it. The bottom line here, is that the 200-day SMA is followed closely by many market participants to determine the state of the overall direction of a particular financial instrument or index.

With such an interest in the 200-day SMA, I was motivated to design a strategy using Fibonacci around these levels. What I came up with was a strategy that identifies moves that are contrary to how the crowd acts on price action around the 200-day SMA. I named this strategy Heisenberg 200 after the Heisenberg Uncertainty Principle. The Heisenberg Uncertainty Principle basically says that in measuring something, we alter it, and that makes the measurement invalid. Could I apply this principle to the markets? In my mind, it was clear that with so many people making decisions to buy or sell based on the general rule I gave above, it would naturally distort the observation and make those buy or sell decisions "obsolete" or inaccurate. Is it a stretch? Conceptually it may sound that way, but the actual trade opportunities speak to the contrary.

What I have done is taken two concepts you have already learned, which are Support and Resistance FibZones and Two-Step Patterns (TSPs), and put them in a melting pot with the 200-day SMA. I was able to create a personal strategy that identifies quite powerful reversal moves.

## BEARISH HEISENBERG 200

Price goes above the 200 Day SMA but completes a Bearish Two Step Pattern (TSP) and hits our resistance FibZone. This initiates a potential short Heisenberg 200 trade.

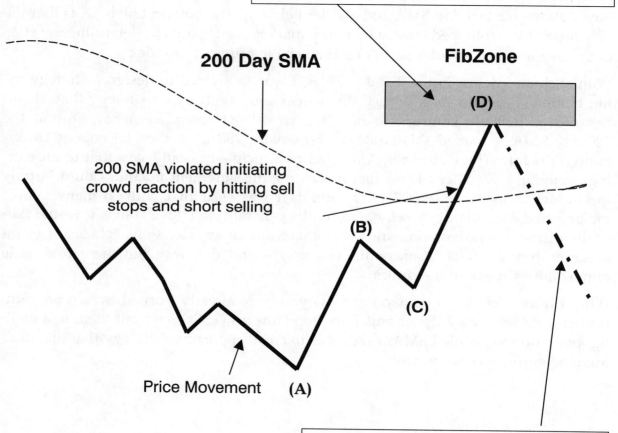

**200 Day SMA**

**FibZone**

(D)

200 SMA violated initiating crowd reaction by hitting sell stops and short selling

(B)

(C)

Price Movement     (A)

Once price reverses down after hitting the resistance FibZone the crowd has to sell longs. In some cases they shift to short selling because price is back below the 200 SMA. This addes fuel for the ride down.

# HEISENBERG 200: RULES

## Rules For Short Sales (Buys Are Reversed):

1.  A bearish Two-Step Pattern has completed. This includes Symmetrical, Gartley, and Butterfly TSPs.

2.  The pattern has hit a Resistance FibZone of at least three Fibonacci price levels.

3.  The final point (D) of the TSP must complete above the 200-day SMA.

4.  Enter a short trade when price goes below the previous day's low. Or, consider a trigger entry from Chapter 11.

5.  Once triggered into a short trade my initial stop is just above the Resistance FibZone.

6.  My first objective on the short trade is the .50 to .618 retracement level of point A to D. Once I have taken profits on half the position at this level I will trail my stop down. Ideally the stop can be moved to breakeven. However, the more important issue is that the stop is trailed down to a recent swing high point.

7.  My second and final objective is the 1.272 extension of swing A:D. Once price hits this Fibonacci level I trail my stop to the previous day's high. Basically what I am trying to do here is allow myself to ride a home run if it happens. Otherwise I've trailed the stop to a point where I've locked in sizeable profits.

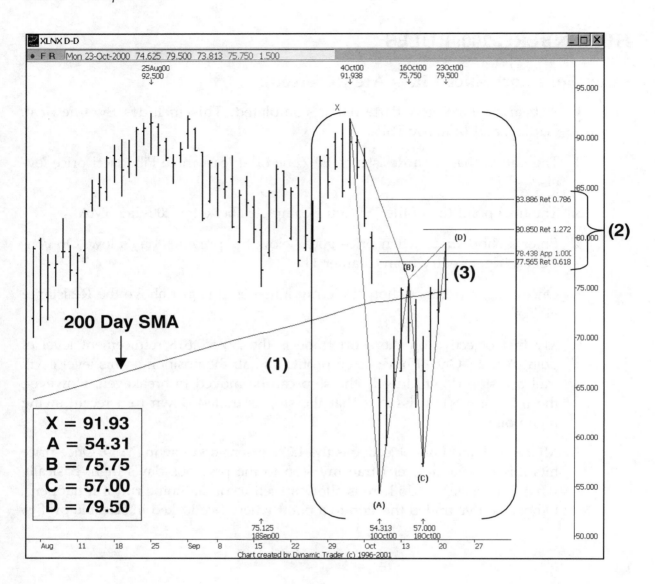

XLNX D-D

F R   Mon 23-Oct-2000  74.625  79.500  73.813  75.750  1.500

X = 91.93
A = 54.31
B = 75.75
C = 57.00
D = 79.50

200 Day SMA

Chart created by Dynamic Trader (c) 1996-2001

## Heisenberg 200 Setup:

Above is a daily chart of Xilinx (XLNX). The necessary ingredients are in place:

1.  A Bearish Gartley TSP Pattern has formed.

2.  A Resistance FibZone of at least three levels has been tested. In this case we have four Fibonacci price resistance levels in our FibZone.

3.  Point D of the pattern completes above the 200-day SMA. So, it's time to look for shorts.

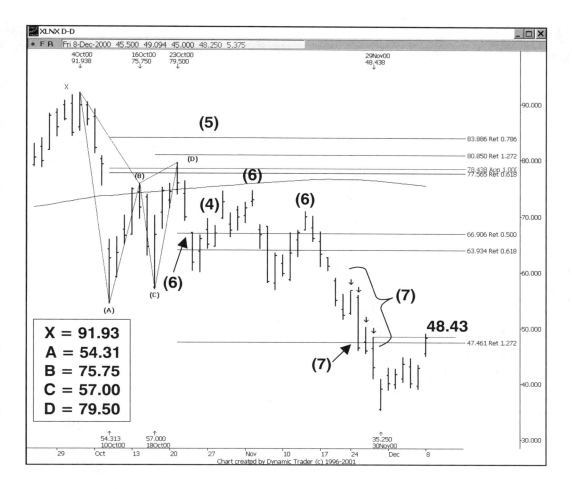

## Heisenberg 200 Result:

4.  After the TSP is complete, a simple trigger would be to take a short trade below the previous bar's low. In this case, I am triggered short at 73.81

5.  My initial stop is just above the resistance zone at 84. This is a 15% difference between my stop and entry price. With such a large price and percentage range, I will reduce my position size to account for this relatively large Resistance FibZone.

6.  The next day, I take profits between 64 and 66, which is the range of the .50 and .618 Fibonacci retracements of low point A to high point D. Price rallies but finds a swing high point and my stop is moved down. I find a couple of swing high points to move my stop to as price falls.

7.  Price finally hits the 1.272 extension of swing A:D at 47.46. I now trail my stop to the previous bar high. Continue to do this as we make new lows. Ultimately I'm stopped out at 48.43 for a 25-point gain.

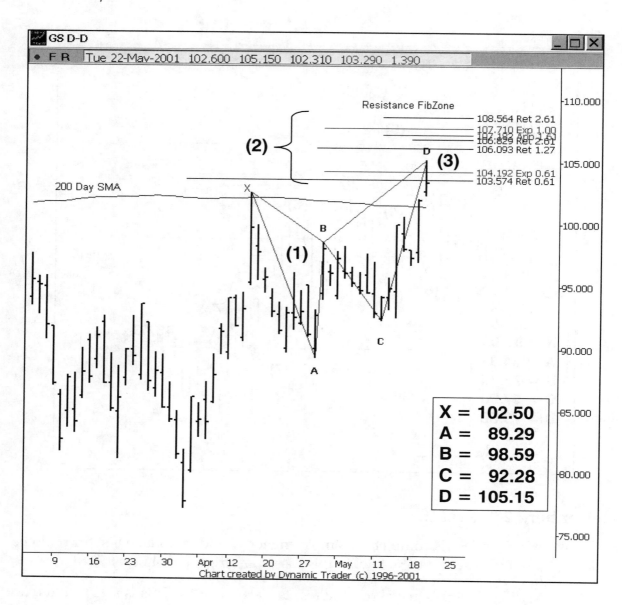

GS D-D

● F R    Tue 22-May-2001  102.600  105.150  102.310  103.290  1.390

Resistance FibZone

108.564 Ret 2.61
107.710 Exp 1.00
106.829 Ret 2.61
106.093 Ret 1.27

(2)

D  (3)

104.192 Exp 0.61
103.574 Ret 0.61

200 Day SMA

X

B

(1)

A

C

X = 102.50
A =  89.29
B =  98.59
C =  92.28
D = 105.15

9   16   23   30   Apr  12   20   27   May  11   18   25
Chart created by Dynamic Trader (c) 1996-2001

## Heisenberg 200 Setup:

Above is a daily chart of Goldman Sachs (GS). The necessary ingredients are in place:

1. A Bearish Butterfly TSP Pattern has formed.

2. A Resistance FibZone of at least three levels has been tested. In this case we have seven Fibonacci price resistance levels in our FibZone.

3. Point D of the pattern completes above the 200-day SMA.

With these ingredients in place, it's time to start looking for short trades.

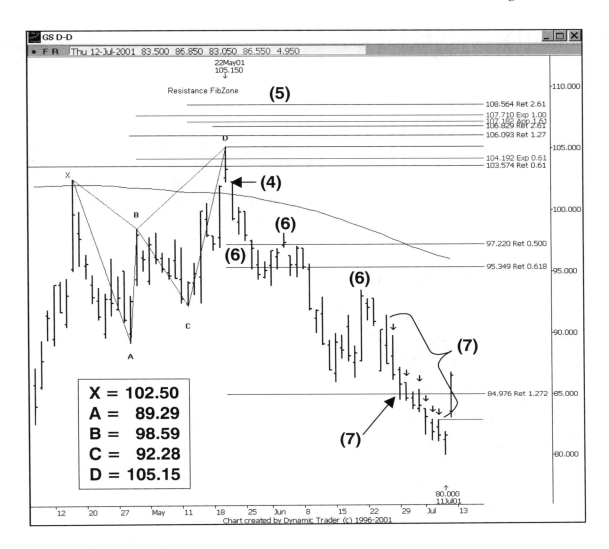

## Heisenberg 200 Result:

4. After the TSP is complete, a simple trigger would be to take a short trade below the previous bar's low. In this case, I am triggered short at 102.30.

5. My initial stop is just above the resistance zone at 108.60.

6. Three days later, I take profits between 95 and 97, which is the range of the .50 and .618 Fibonacci retracements of low point A to high point D. Price rallies but finds a swing high point and my stop is moved down. I find a couple of swing high points to move my stop to as price falls.

7. Price finally hits the 1.272 extension of swing A:D at 84.97. I now trail my stop to the previous bar high. Continue to do this as we make new lows. Ultimately, I'm stopped out around 83.50 for almost 20 points of gain.

# BULLISH HEISENBERG 200

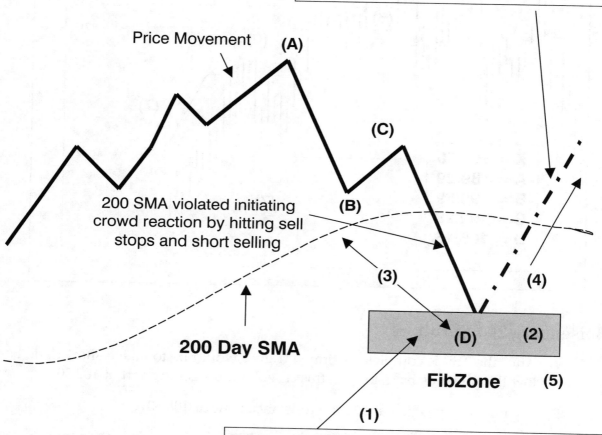

Once price reverses up after hitting the support FibZone the crowd has to cover shorts and be buyers again because price is back above the 200-Day SMA providing fuel for the ride up.

Price Movement

(A)

(C)

(B)

200 SMA violated initiating crowd reaction by hitting sell stops and short selling

(3)

(4)

200 Day SMA

(D)    (2)

FibZone    (5)

(1)

Price goes below 200-Day SMA but completes a Bullish Two-Step Pattern (TSP) and hits our support FibZone and initiates a potential long Heisenberg 200 trade.

## Rules For Buys (Shorts Are Reversed):

1.  A Bullish Two-Step Pattern has been completed. This includes Symmetrical, Gartley, and Butterfly TSPs.

2.  The pattern has hit a Support FibZone of at least three Fibonacci price levels.

3.  The final point (D) of the TSP must complete below the 200-day SMA.

4.  Enter a long trade when price goes above the previous day's high. Or, consider a trigger entry from Chapter 11.

5.  Once triggered into a long trade, my initial stop is just below the Support FibZone.

6.  My first objective on the long trade is the .50 to .618 retracement level of point A to D. Once I have taken profits on half the position at this level, I will trail my stop up. Ideally the stop can be moved to breakeven. However, the more important issue is that the stop is trailed up to a recent swing low point.

7.  My second and final objective is the 1.272 extension of swing A:D. I do not immediately take profits at this level. Once price hits this Fibonacci level, I trail my stop to the previous day's low. As higher highs are made, I continue to trail the stop to the previous bar's low. Basically what I am trying to do here is allow myself to ride a home run if it happens. Otherwise I've trailed the stop to a point where I've locked in sizeable profits.

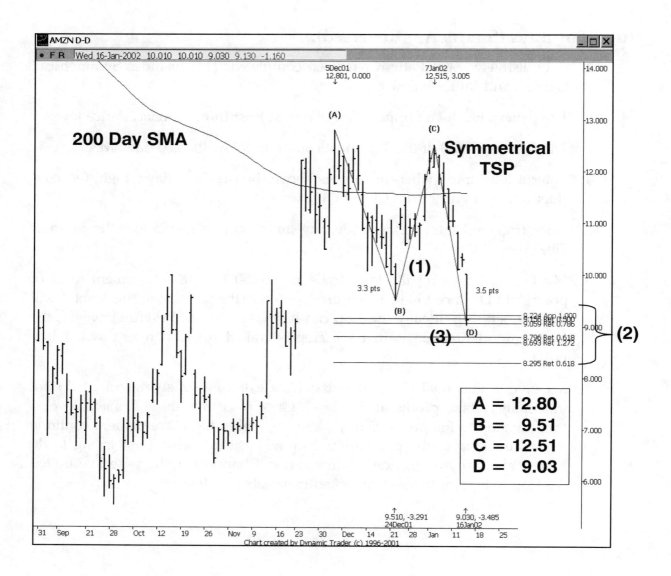

AMZN D-D

F R   Wed 16-Jan-2002  10.010  10.010  9.030  9.130  -1.160

200 Day SMA

5Dec01
12.801, 0.000

7Jan02
12.515, 3.005

(A)

(C)

Symmetrical
TSP

(1)

3.3 pts        3.5 pts

(B)

(3)        (D)

9.224 App 1.000
9.156 Ret 0.500
9.059 Ret 0.786
8.796 Ret 0.618
8.693 Ret 1.272
8.295 Ret 0.618

(2)

A = 12.80
B =  9.51
C = 12.51
D =  9.03

9.510, -3.291
24Dec01

9.030, -3.485
16Jan02

31  Sep  21  28  Oct  12  19  26  Nov  9  16  23  30  Dec  14  21  28  Jan  11  18  25

Chart created by Dynamic Trader (c) 1996-2001

## Heisenberg 200 Setup:

Above is a daily chart of Amazon.com (AMZN). The necessary ingredients are in place:

1. A Bullish Symmetrical TSP Pattern has formed.

2. A Support FibZone of at least three levels has been tested. In this case we have six Fibonacci price support levels in our FibZone.

3. Point D of the pattern crosses and completes below the 200-day SMA.

At this point it's time to start looking for opportunities to go long.

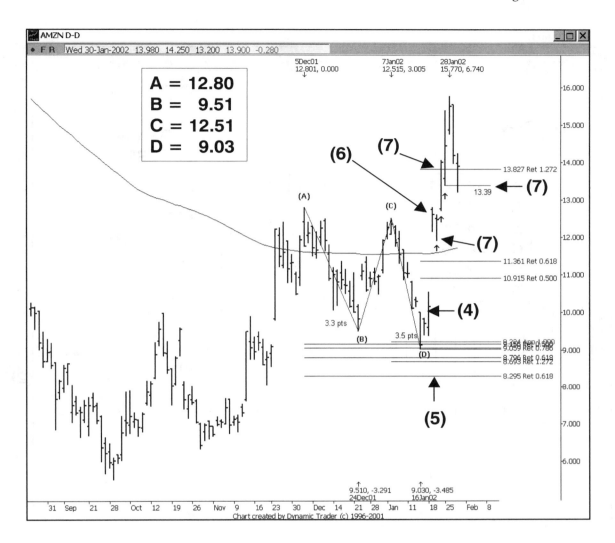

A = 12.80
B =  9.51
C = 12.51
D =  9.03

## Heisenberg 200 Result:

4. After the TSP is complete, a simple trigger would be to take a long trade above the previous bar's high. In this case I am triggered long at 9.85.

5. My initial stop is just below the support zone at 8.25.

6. The next day I take profits at the open between 12 and 13, because price gapped above range of the .50 and .618 Fibonacci retracements of low point A to high point D.

7. Price declines one day then rallies to hit the 1.272 extension of swing A:D at 13.82. I now trail my stop to the previous bar low. Continue to do this as we make new highs. Ultimately I'm stopped out around 13.39 for almost 3.5 points of gains on a nine-dollar stock.

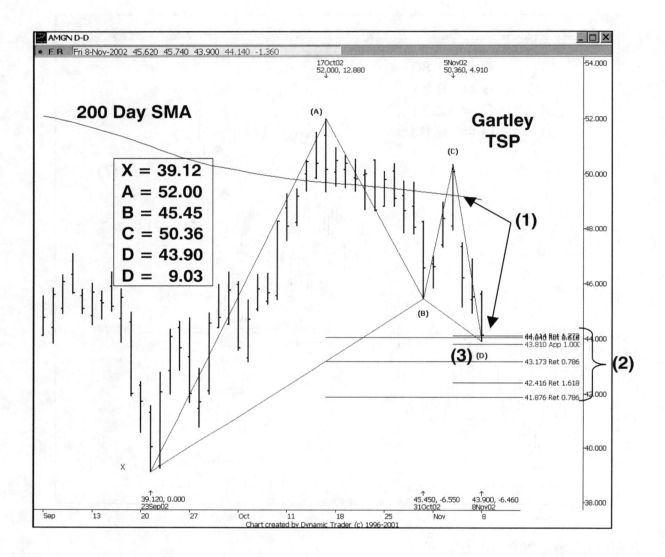

Above is a daily chart of Amgen.com (AMGN). The necessary ingredients are in place:

1.  A Bullish Symmetrical TSP Pattern has formed. It looks like price has given up and is ready to fall apart after testing the 200-day SMA twice. I think Heisenberg has something else in store.

2.  A Support FibZone of at least three levels has been tested. In this case we have six Fibonacci price support levels in our FibZone.

3.  Point D of the pattern completes below the 200-day SMA. So, it's time to look for longs.

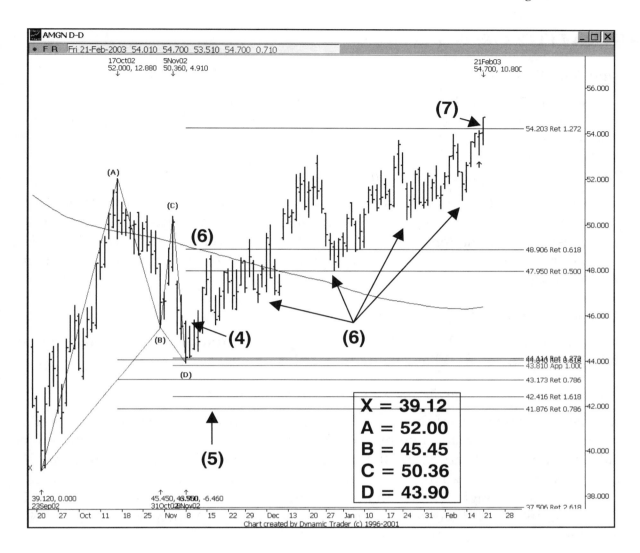

## Heisenberg 200 Result:

4.  After the TSP is complete, a simple trigger would be to take a long trade above the previous bar's high. In this case I am triggered long at 45.53.

5.  My initial stop is just below the support zone at 41.70.

6.  In a few days the first objective between 48 and 49 was hit, which is between the .50 and .618 Fibonacci retracements of high point A to low point D. AMGN continues to make higher swing lows to trail the stop up as we approach the 1.272 retracement of swing A:D.

7.  As of this writing, AMGN is still an active position (with only half of the original trade remaining after taking profits around $48) and has just hit the 1.272 extension so the stop was trailed up to the previous bar's low.

## STRATEGY Q&A

*Question:* What makes this different than simply trading the TSP patterns?

*Answer:* The 200-day SMA is adding market participants and increasing volatility. So, if the "crowd" is caught on the wrong side, then our TSP patterns can create even more significant trading opportunities.

*Question:* What is a good way to scan for these setups?

*Answer:* The two things I look for are stocks with liquidity and stocks around the 200-day SMA. So volume and the moving average is all you need. Once a watch list is established, it's a matter of waiting for patterns to develop. But the one thing nice about this strategy is that there is always a pipeline of stocks approaching their 200-day SMA.

*Question:* Do you trade this strategy on any other time frame?

*Answer:* I do not. The 200-day SMA is for daily charts. You could shift to a 40-period SMA on a weekly chart. I have never traded this on intraday charts.

*Question:* Are you looking for anything else with these setups?

*Answer:* I do look to see if the setup is occurring within the context of the trend. For example, if we have made two or three higher swing lows and higher swing highs and price pokes its head above the 200-day SMA then falls back and forms a TSP, then I'm more excited about that setup than a stock that is simply in "chop" mode not really making higher highs and higher lows. A mechanical way to scan for this is by using the ADX. I would recommend a 13-period ADX greater than 20 and rising. The ADX is just telling us the strength of the trend, not the direction.

CHAPTER **9**

# SHARK ATTACK

# STRATEGY #6: SHARK ATTACK

At any one time, a Great White has more than 3000 serrated razor-sharp teeth aligned in rows. The Great White is the only shark that will poke its head out of water, possibly to get a view of its prey before attacking. They've also been known to completely jump out of water usually when racing upwards from deep water to catch a fast-moving meal. I don't know about you, but this sounds to me like the market, in many ways.

Whether I'm looking at an intraday, daily, weekly, or monthly chart, I've observed an interesting relationship around swing high or low points. When price is approaching the most recent swing high or low point, it faces a key decision at the .786 retracement level. If the .786 retracement is violated, then price will more often than not continue quickly to the next Fibonacci levels between the 1.272 and 1.618 extension. Although that is a critical part of the Shark Attack strategy, it is not the opportunity I'm looking at. To the untrained eye, it would suggest further downside when a low point is violated and further upside when a high point is violated. This is where the shark attacks. It comes out of the water with power, but once it "attacks," it slides back into the water. Sliding back into the water in trading terms translates to a reversal. That slightly lower low or slightly higher high is a trap, in a sense. Yes, this description sounds a lot like double tops and bottoms. In a sense, it is. However, key points to remember that the general double top and double bottom discussion do not include are:

1. What the relationship is between the .786 and the extension levels at swing points.

2. Hitting extension levels like the 1.272 and 1.618 of previous swings represent "stretched" price action and a tradable Shark Attack reversal typically occurs around these extension levels.

3. The more Fibonacci extension levels that come together in a tight price range, the greater the likelihood for a tradable reversal.

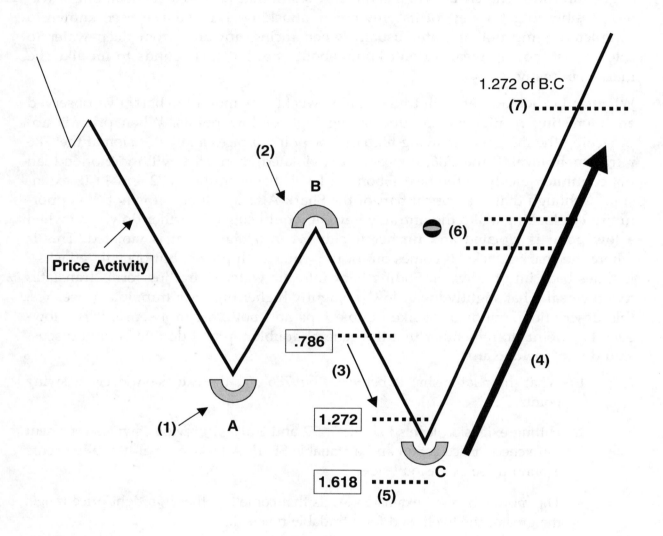

Shark Attack—Long Setup

Price Activity

(1) A

(2) B

.786

(3)

1.272

1.618 (5)

C

(6)

(4)

1.272 of B:C

(7)

## Rules For Buys (Shorts Are Reversed):

1. Swing point low A is identified.

2. Once a low point A is established, price rallies to form a high point B.

3. This is where it gets interesting. As price approaches the .786 retracement of swing A:B, a potential momentum trade is setting up. Basically, if price goes below the .786, it is likely to decline to the 1.272 to 1.618 extension of swing A:B. Many times, this move from the .786 to the extension levels happens very quickly. So this presents short-term momentum traders an opportunity. This opportunity is peanuts though, compared to the reversal potential.

4. Once price goes down to the range of the 1.272 to 1.618 Fibonacci extensions, it forms a shark-looking formation. It's like the shark is getting ready to take a bite out of any short traders at this new low level as price reverses from these extension levels and rallies significantly to the upside. Go long on a trade above the previous bar high.

5. Initial stop below the Support FibZone.

6. The first objective on this trade is the .50 to .618 retracement of swing B:C.

7. The next objective is the 1.272 extension of B:C. Once this price level is hit, begin trailing a stop to the previous bar low on the rest of the position.

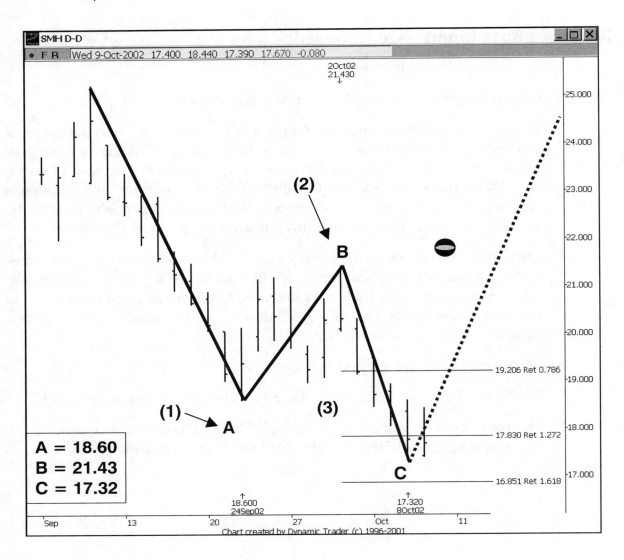

## Shark Attack Long Setup:

1. Low point A is made.

2. Once a low point A is established, price rallies to form a high point B.

3. Price goes below 19.20, which is the .786 retracement. This presents a short momentum trade opportunity down to the 1.272 to 1.618 extension of swing A:B. In two bars, SMH hits 17.83 for a quick potential profit of a little over 1 point.

Once price hits the 1.272 to 1.618 extension of swing A:B, we have a Shark Attack pattern in full swing. With a new low established, the shorts are in control, or they think that's the case, until the shark takes a bite out of them.

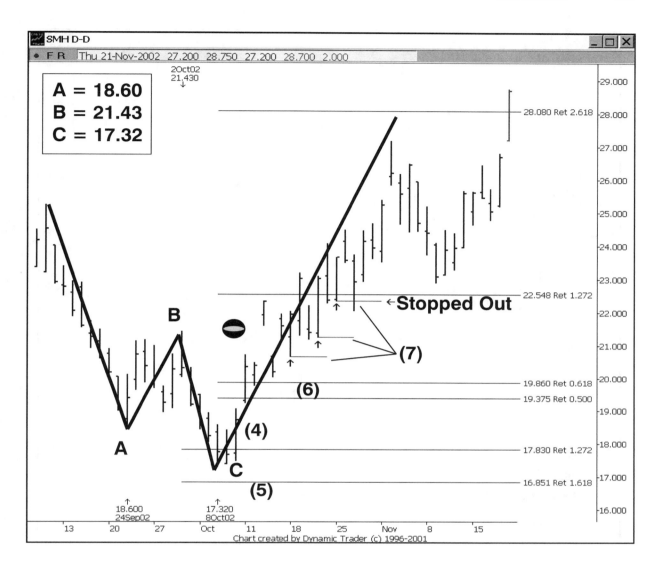

## Shark Attack Long Result:

4. A long trade is initiated at 18.45 when we get the first price bar to go above the previous day's high after hitting our Fibonacci extension levels.

5. The initial stop loss order is placed just below the 1.618 extension level around 16.80.

6. The first objective on half of the position is between the .50 and .618 retracement of the high point B to low point C.

7. The next objective is for price to hit the 1.272 extension of swing B:C. This level comes in at 22.54. As the stock makes new highs, I move the stop up to the previous bar's low. In this case, we are stopped out at 22.35.

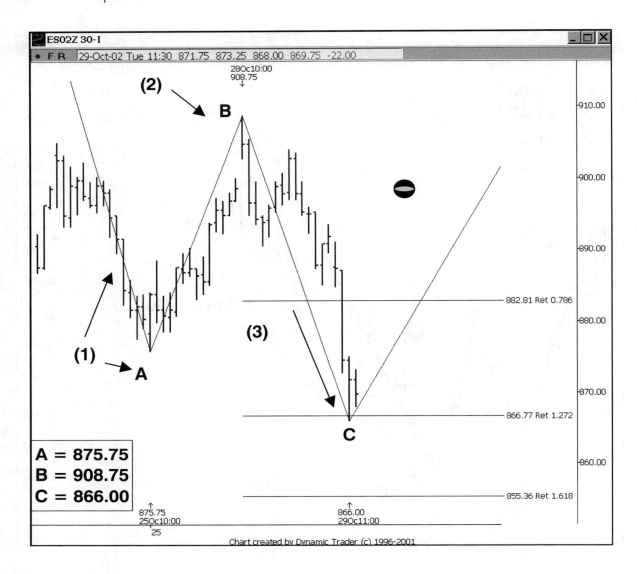

## Shark Attack Long Setup:

1.  A downtrend is in place as the stock forms swing point A.

2.  Once a low point A is established, price rallies to form a high point B.

3.  Price goes below 882.75, which is the .786 retracement of A:B. This presents a short momentum trade opportunity. In two 30-minute bars, the S&P 500 e-Mini futures contract trades down 16 points without looking back. Once price hits the 1.272 to 1.618 extension of swing A:B, we have a Shark Attack pattern in full swing. With a new low established the shorts are in control, or they think that's the case until the shark takes a bite out of them.

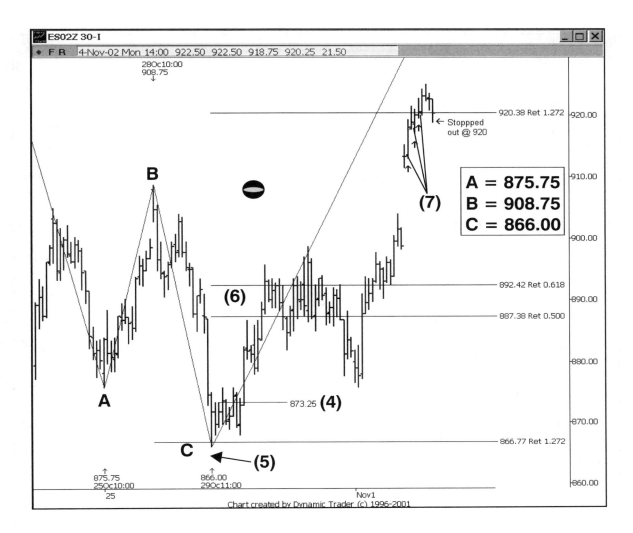

## Shark Attack Long Result:

4. A long trade is initiated at 873.25 when we get the first price bar to go above the previous day's high after hitting our Fibonacci extension levels.

5. The initial stop loss order is placed just below the 1.618 extension level around 855.50. If this is too far, consider placing the stop just below the low made into the extension area before triggering long. In this case, that would be 865.75.

6. The first objective on half of the position is between the .50 and .618 retracement of the high point B to low point C.

7. The next objective is for price to hit the 1.272 extension of swing B:C. This level comes in at 920.25. As the stock makes new highs I move the stop up to the previous bar's low. In this case, we are stopped out at 920.00.

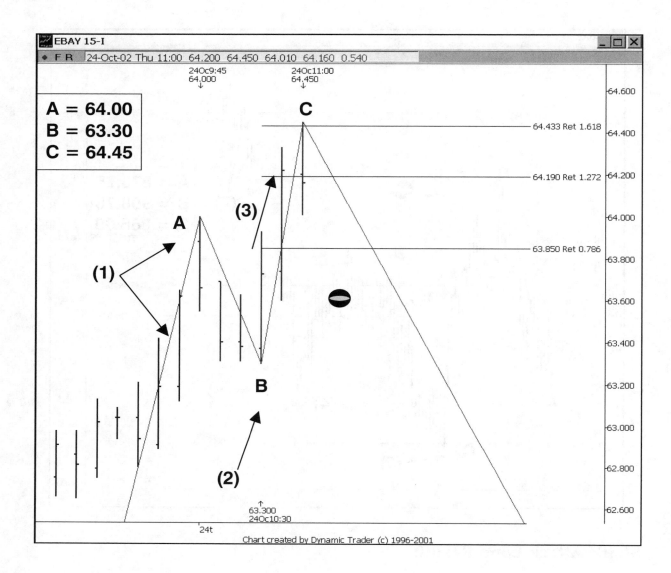

**A = 64.00**
**B = 63.30**
**C = 64.45**

## Shark Attack Short Setup:

1.  An up trend is in place as the stock forms swing point A.

2.  Once a high point A is established, price declines to form a low point B.

3.  Price goes above 63.85, which is the .786 retracement of A:B. This presents a long momentum trade opportunity. In two 15-minute bars, EBAY trades up almost .30 points without looking back. Once price hits the 1.272 to 1.618 extension of swing A:B, we have a Shark Attack pattern in full swing. With a new high established, the longs think they are in control. Unfortunately they are buying in shark-infested waters.

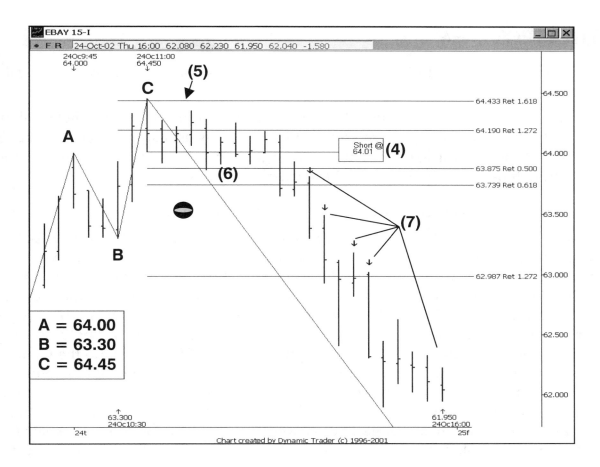

## Shark Attack Short Result:

4. A short trade is initiated at 64.01 when we get the first price bar to go below the previous bar's low, after hitting our Fibonacci extension levels.

5. The initial stop loss order is placed just above the 1.618 extension level around 64.50.

6. The first objective on half of the position is between the .50 and .618 retracement of the high point B to low point C. In a situation like this when using intraday charts, I will sometimes not take profits and just wait for the 1.272 extension level.

7. The 1.272 extension of swing B:C comes in at 62.98. Once price hits this level I start trailing my stop to the previous bar's high. As the stock makes new lows, I move the stop down to the previous bar's high. In this case we are not stopped out at the end of the day, so I close the position because the trade was based on a 15-minute chart. So, the short was covered around 62.50 for approximately a 2-point profit intraday.

# STRATEGY Q&A

*Question:* *This looks a lot like a double top/double bottom strategy. Is that what you are defining?*

*Answer:* In theory, yes, the double tops and bottoms can make slightly higher highs or slightly lower lows. I suppose you could look at this as a specific type of double top or bottom with a specific Fibonacci target completion point for the second peak/trough between the 1.272 and 1.618 extension levels.

*Question:* *Again, could you explain exactly why you call it "shark attack"?*

*Answer:* Sure. Let's talk in terms of a Shark Attack short setup. When you look at this pattern as it is forming, price establishes the first high point. Then it reverses in the opposite direction to the downside. This gives "hope" to the early reversal traders looking for a nice downside move. However, when price returns to the previous high and makes a slightly higher high, then the early reversal traders typically get stopped out and are forced to buy to cover their short position. Not only do early reversal traders get stopped out, but this pulls new trend followers into the game as a new high is established. This influx of long order flow creates momentum and will typically push price to a Fibonacci extension level between 1.272 to 1.618 of swing A:B as we defined earlier in this chapter. Many times this is the "last gasp" exhaustion move before the real change of direction occurs. When you look at a chart this price movement takes the shape of a shark head with its mouth open. Basically, the shark is "attacking."

*Question:* *As a Shark Attack pattern completes, are there any specific characteristics about the FibZone that one should look for?*

*Answer:* I like to see multiple extension levels fall into this FibZone from various low to high or high to low swings. Specifically, multiple levels of the 1.272 and 1.618 ratios. When four or more extension levels come together, there is an extremely high probability for at least a short-term tradable reversal.

# CHAPTER 10

# AIR POCKETS

# STRATEGY #7: AIR POCKETS

One of my favorite technical analysis tools is the Average Directional Index (ADX). In short, it is a tool that helps determine the strength or lack of strength in a chart's trend. By combining this tool with Support and Resistance FibZones, I have created a couple of strategies that take advantage of gaps between FibZones. The two types of Air Pockets we will discuss are Reversal Air Pockets (RAPS) and the second one we will discuss are Continuation Air Pockets (CAPS). These trades all fall along the lines of momentum trading as a trader is looking to go long the violation of a Resistance FibZone and to short a violation of a Support FibZone. Let's first look at the Reversal Air Pockets.

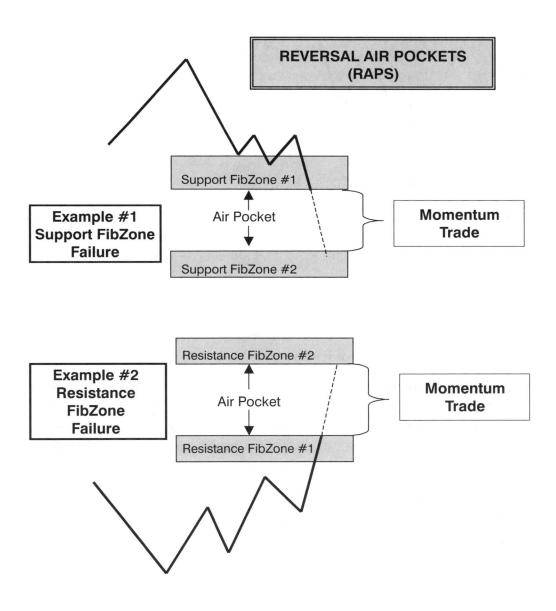

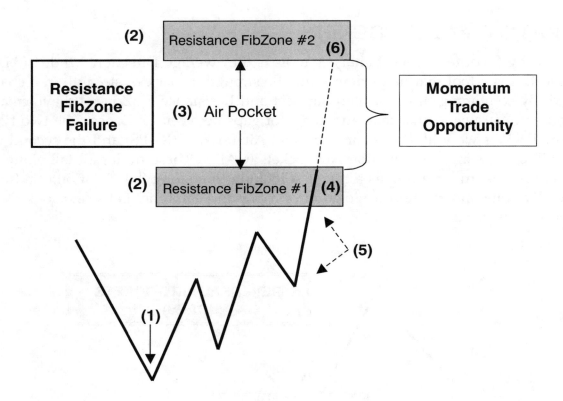

## Rules For Buys (Shorts Are Reversed):

1. Price has been trending down and has just established a low point where the 14-period ADX is greater than 20. This is where we calculate Fibonacci price resistance levels using retracements, extensions, projections, and expansions.

2. After calculating Fibonacci price resistance levels, two Resistance FibZones are identified. FibZone #1 is closest to current price.

3. There must be a tradable gap "Air Pocket" between the two zones, where no Fibonacci price resistance levels exist.

4. Price trades up to FibZone #1 and pushes through the highest level in this zone as the 14-period ADX reading goes below 20. At this point there are two possible entry options. First, the trader could enter immediately upon violation of the zone. Second, the trader could wait for a small pullback to test the zone that was just broken, then look to be a buyer.

5. Initial stop loss orders could be placed below FibZone #1, the current bar (the bar that violates FibZone #1), or previous bar low.

6. Objective on this trade is up to Resistance FibZone #2.

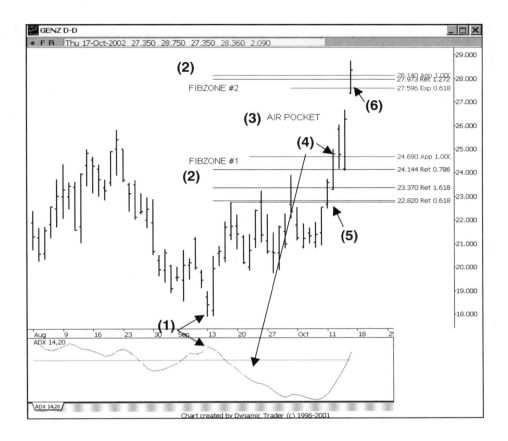

## Reversal Air Pockets: Long

1. Price establishes a swing low point where the 14-period ADX is above 20. At this point we calculate Fibonacci price resistance levels.

2. Two Resistance FibZones are identified.

3. There are over 5 points of "Air Pocket" between FibZone #1 and FibZone #2 which should provide plenty of opportunity if FibZone #1 is violated to the upside.

4. As price trades up, the ADX drops below 20. Price moves up to the zone and pushes through and a possible long entry is made just above 24.69. (Note: the next day GENZ gaps up, but comes back to test the FibZone it has just cleared. This is another entry opportunity.)

5. A stop is placed at the lower of a) the bottom of FibZone #1 or b) the low prior to the day price trades above the FibZone. In this case the two are about the same so my stop is just below 22.82.

6. The objective on the trade is 27.59, which is the bottom of FibZone #2.

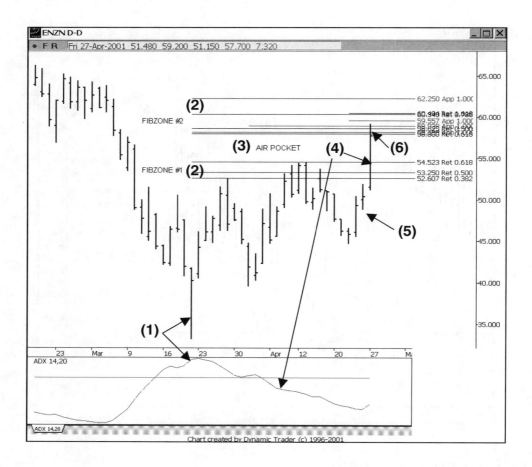

## Reversal Air Pockets: Long

1. Price establishes a swing low point where the 14-period ADX is above 20. At this point we calculate Fibonacci price resistance levels.

2. Two Resistance FibZones are identified.

3. There is over 3.5 points of "Air Pocket" or profit potential, between FibZone #1 and FibZone #2, which should provide plenty of opportunity if FibZone #1 is violated to the upside.

4. As price trades up, the ADX drops below 20. Price moves up to the zone and pushes through and a possible long entry is made just above 54.52. (Note: a pullback opportunity never occurred as ENZN hits the Air Pocket and our objective of 58.00 all in the same day.)

5. A stop is placed below the previous day's low. This is a wide stop and I would consider moving the stop up to the current day's low.

6. The objective on the trade is 58.00, which is the bottom of FibZone #2.

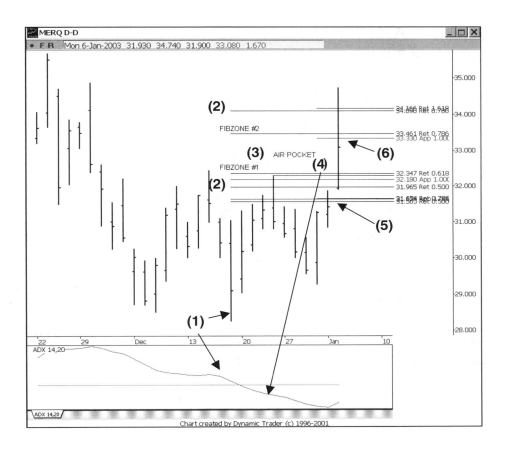

## Reversal Air Pockets: Long

1.  Price establishes a swing low point where the 14-period ADX is above 20. At this point we calculate Fibonacci price resistance levels.

2.  Two Resistance FibZones are identified.

3.  There is an Air Pocket of approximately 1 point of profit potential between FibZone #1 and FibZone #2.

4.  As price trades up, the ADX drops below 20. Price moves up to the zone and pushes through and a possible long entry is made just above 32.34.

5.  A stop is placed below FibZone #1 around 31.50.

6.  Once again, price jumps through the Air Pocket the same day that it pushes through FibZone #1. I find many of the powerful Air Pocket moves occur when there are one or more high points that have tested the upper level of FibZone #1 prior to the actual bar in which the FibZone is violated. These high points make the top of our FibZone even more critical and when violated, explosive opportunity.

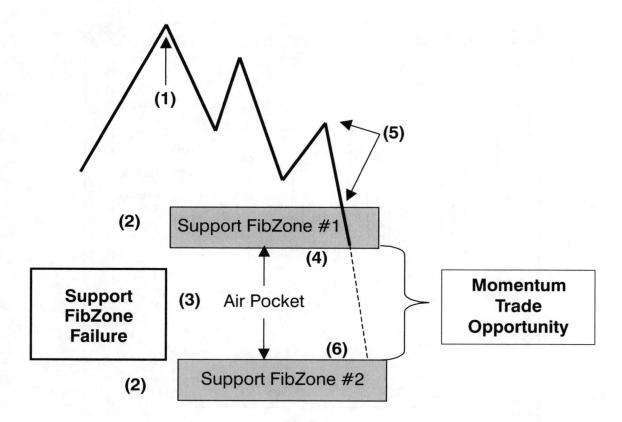

## Rules For Shorts (Buys Are Reversed):

1. Price has established a high point where the 14-period ADX is greater than 20. This is where we calculate Fibonacci price support levels using retracements, extensions, projections, and expansions.

2. After calculating Fibonacci price support levels, two Support FibZones are identified.

3. There must be a tradable gap "Air Pocket" between the two zones where no Fibonacci price support levels exist.

4. Price trades down to FibZone #1 as the 14-period ADX crosses below 20. At this point there are two possible entry options. First, the trader could enter immediately upon violation of the zone. Second, the trader could wait for a small pullback to test the zone that was just broken, then look to short.

5. Consider three stop placement areas based on the current day being the day price violates FibZone #1: a) current bar high; b) previous bar high; c) highest price level in FibZone #1.

6. Objective on this trade is down to Support FibZone #2.

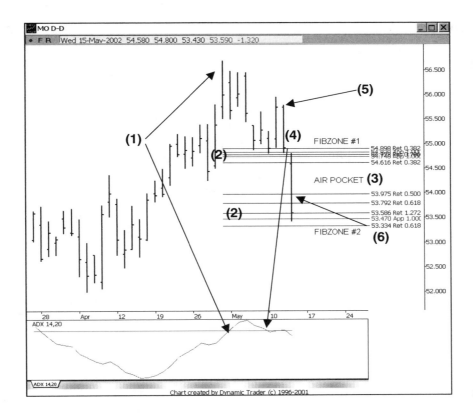

## Reversal Air Pockets: Short

1.  Price establishes a swing high point where the 14-period ADX is above 20. At this point we calculate Fibonacci price support levels.

2.  Two Support FibZones are identified.

3.  There is an Air Pocket of approximately 70 cents of profit potential between FibZone #1 and FibZone #2.

4.  As price trades down, the ADX drops below 20. Price moves down to the FibZone and pushes through and a possible short entry is made just below 54.61.

5.  A stop is placed above the previous bar high around 55.75.

6.  Price drops like a stone through our Air Pocket the same day that it pushes through FibZone #1. I find many of the powerful Air Pocket moves occur when there are one or more low points that have tested the lower levels of FibZone #1 prior to the actual bar in which the FibZone is violated. These low points make the bottom of our FibZone even more critical and when violated, explosive opportunity.

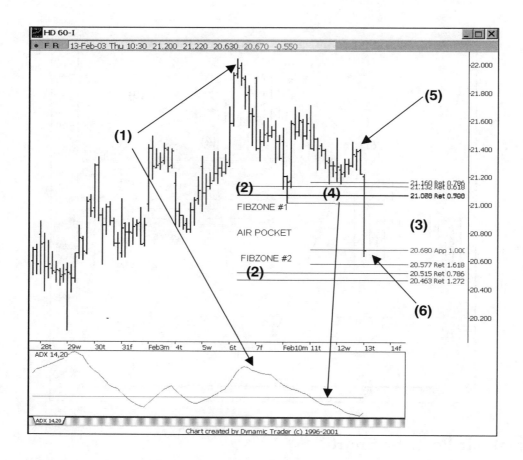

## Reversal Air Pockets: Short

1.  Price establishes a swing high point on this 60-minute chart of HD where the 14-period ADX is above 20. At this point, we calculate Fibonacci price support levels.

2.  Two Support FibZones are identified.

3.  There is an Air Pocket of approximately 40 cents of profit potential between FibZone #1 and FibZone #2.

4.  As price trades down, the ADX drops below 20. Price moves down to the FibZone and pushes through and a possible short entry is made just below 21.06.

5.  A stop is placed above the previous bar high around 21.40.

6.  Price hits the objective in the same bar that it pushes through FibZone #1.

All that for $.40? Yes, in fact, let's look at it in percentage terms. That's a 2% return in 60 minutes.

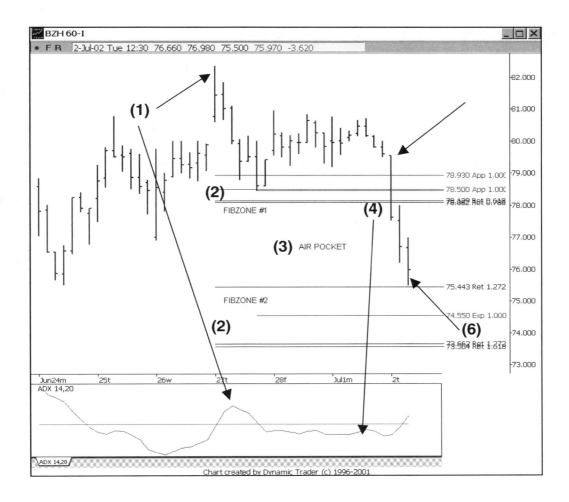

## Reversal Air Pockets: Short

1. Price establishes a swing high point on this 60-minute chart of BZH, where the 14-period ADX is above 20. At this point we calculate Fibonacci price support levels.

2. Two Support FibZones are identified.

3. There is an Air Pocket of approximately 2.60 points of profit potential, between FibZone #1 and FibZone #2.

4. As price trades down, the ADX drops below 20. Price moves down to the FibZone and pushes through and a possible short entry is made just below 78.06.

5. A stop is placed above the previous bar high around 79.50.

6. Three hours later, price hits the objective around 75.45.

## CONTINUATION AIR POCKETS (CAPS)

Air Pockets exist regardless of trend, but the most profitable and consistent Air Pockets I've found are either in the Reversal Air Pocket (RAPS) strategy or in this Continuation Air Pocket (CAPS) strategy. The difference between the two is quite simple. In the case of a short trade CAPS setup, I want to see price in a downtrend as it comes into the first Support FibZone. For long trades, I want to see price already in an uptrend as it hits our first Resistance FibZone. I will also specify the ADX requirements for each setup as we dig in. For the most part, it's a matter of where price was coming from prior to hitting the FibZones that determines whether it's a reversal or continuation Air Pocket.

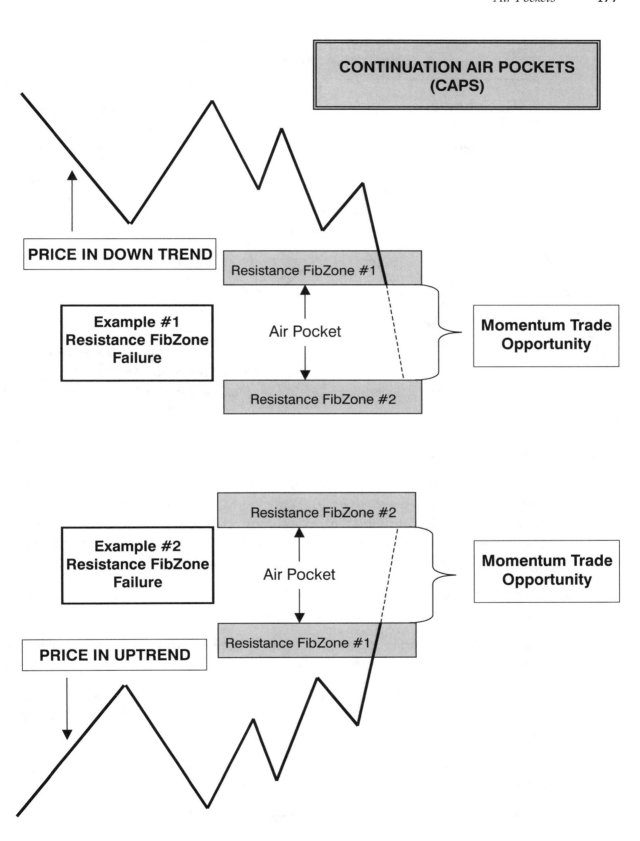

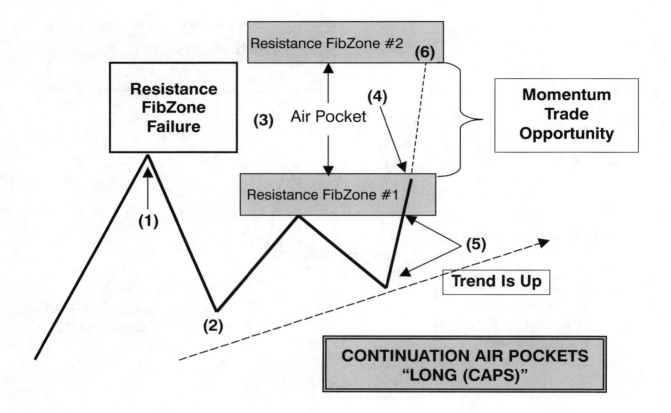

**Rules For Buys (Shorts Are Reversed):**

1. Price has been trending up and has just established a high point where the 14-period ADX is greater than 20. With the Reversal Air Pockets, this would be where we calculate Fibonacci price support levels. Not here. In this situation we wait for price to trade down and make a low point and start to rally again. Now we calculate Fibonacci price resistance levels from point (2).

2. After calculating Fibonacci price resistance levels, two Resistance FibZones are identified. FibZone #1 is closest to current price.

3. There must be a tradable gap "Air Pocket" between the two zones, where no Fibonacci price resistance levels exist.

4. Price pushes through the highest level in FibZone #1 as the ADX has dropped below 20. A long trade can be placed just above FibZone #1 or wait for price to come back and test FibZone #1.

5. Initial stop loss orders could be placed below FibZone #1, the current bar (the bar that violates FibZone #1), or previous the bar low.

6. Objective on this trade is up to Resistance FibZone #2.

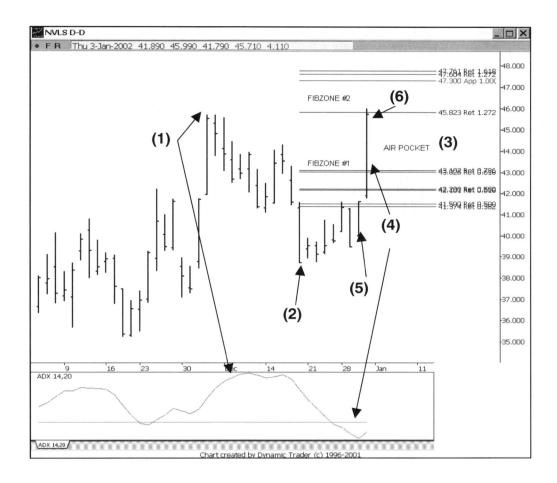

## Continuation Air Pockets (CAPS): Long

1. Price establishes a swing high point where the 14-period ADX is above 20. This just means there is at least a moderately strong trend in place.

2. Instead of calculating Fibonacci price support levels, wait for a swing low to be completed. Now, let's calculate Fibonacci price resistance levels using retracements, extensions, projections, and expansions.

3. There are over 2.7 points of "Air Pocket" between FibZone #1 and FibZone #2, which should provide plenty of opportunity if FibZone #1 is violated to the upside.

4. As price trades back up, the ADX drops below 20. Price moves up to the zone and pushes through and a possible long entry is made just above 43.10.

5. A stop is placed around $40, which is the previous bar's low.

6. Our objective is hit the same day we are filled for a 2.7 point gain.

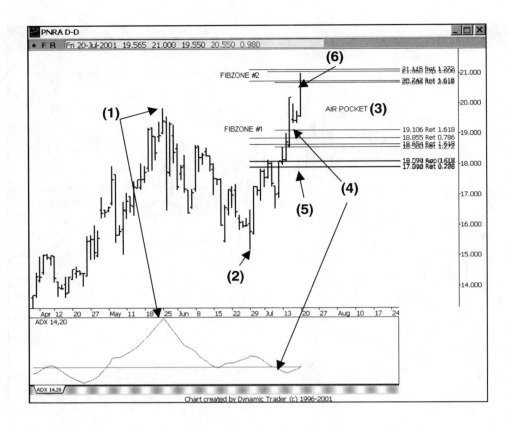

## Continuation Air Pockets (CAPS): Long

1.  Price establishes a swing high point where the 14-period ADX is above 20. This just means there is at least a moderately strong trend in place.

2.  Instead of calculating Fibonacci price support levels, wait for a swing low to be completed. Now, let's calculate Fibonacci price resistance levels using retracements, extensions, projections, and expansions.

3.  There are over 1.5 points of "Air Pocket" between FibZone #1 and FibZone #2, which should provide plenty of opportunity if FibZone #1 is violated to the upside.

4.  ADX drops below 20. Price moves up to the zone and pushes through and a possible long entry is made just above 19.10.

5.  A stop is placed just under FibZone #1 around 17.85.

6.  The first day was a large thrust above the zone, then a couple days of consolidation and a final thrust to hit our objective. I really don't like to see much time go by where price goes sideways, two or three bars at most, before I start to consider cashing in and moving on.

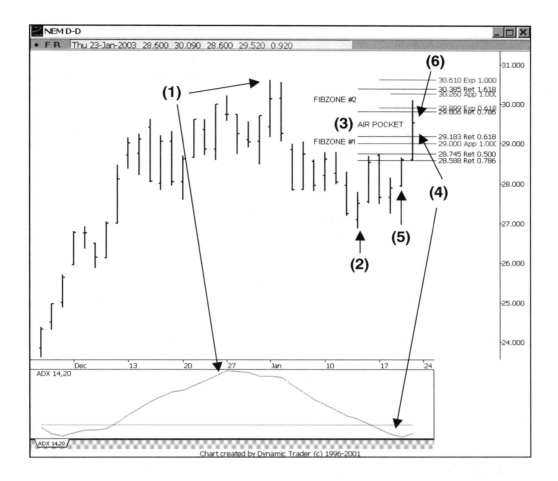

## Continuation Air Pockets (CAPS): Long

1. Price establishes a swing high point where the 14-period ADX is above 20. This just means there is at least a moderately strong trend in place.

2. Instead of calculating Fibonacci price support levels, wait for a swing low to be completed. Now, let's calculate Fibonacci price resistance levels using retracements, extensions, projections, and expansions.

3. There are over $.60 of "Air Pocket" between FibZone #1 and FibZone #2, which should provide opportunity if FibZone #1 is violated to the upside.

4. As price trades back up, the ADX drops below 20. Price moves up to the zone and pushes through and a possible long entry is made just above 29.18.

5. A stop is placed just below $28.00, which is the previous bar's low.

6. Although the size of the profit potential is not fantastic, it is a setup that seems to hit with a very high accuracy rate.

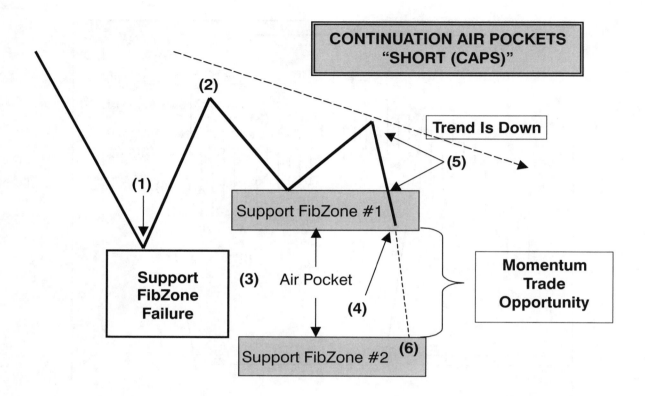

## Rules For Shorts (Buys Are Reversed):

1. Price has been trending down and has just established a low point where the 14-period ADX is greater than 20. With the Reversal Air Pockets, this would be where we calculate Fibonacci price resistance levels. Not here. In this situation we wait for price to trade up and make a high point and start to decline again. As we start to decline again, it is time to calculate Fibonacci price support levels from point (2).

2. After calculating Fibonacci price support levels, two Support FibZones are identified. FibZone #1 is closest to current price.

3. There must be a tradable gap "Air Pocket" between the two zones where no Fibonacci price support levels exist.

4. Price pushes through the lowest level in FibZone #1 as the ADX has dropped below 20. A short trade can be placed just below FibZone #1 or wait for price to come back and test FibZone #1.

5. Initial stop loss orders could be placed above FibZone #1, the current bar high (the bar that violates FibZone #1), or the prior the bar high.

6. Objective on this trade is down to Support FibZone #2.

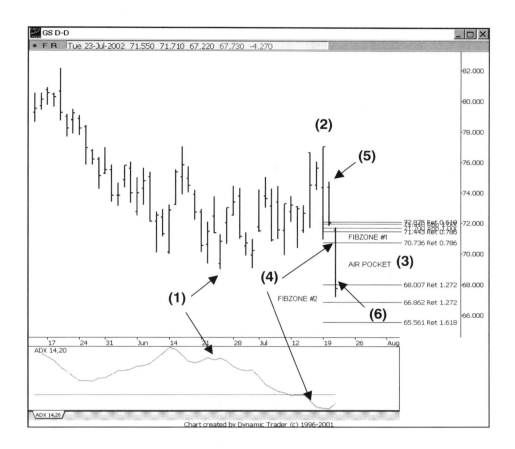

## Continuation Air Pockets (CAPS): Short

1. Price establishes a swing low point where the 14-period ADX is above 20. This just means there is at least a moderately strong trend in place.

2. Instead of calculating Fibonacci price resistance levels, wait for a swing high to be completed. Now, let's calculate Fibonacci price support levels using retracements, extensions, projections, and expansions.

3. There are over 2.7 points of "Air Pocket" between FibZone #1 and FibZone #2, which should provide a very nice opportunity if FibZone #1 is violated to the downside.

4. As price trades back down from point (2), the ADX drops below 20. Price moves down and through FibZone #1 and a possible short entry is made just below 70.73.

5. A stop is placed just above $74, which is the previous bar's high.

6. These are the nice juicy setups. The same day this short is triggered, we have closed out the position for a possible 2.7 point gain.

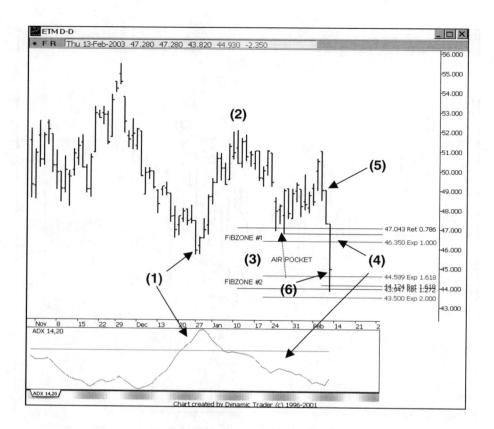

## Continuation Air Pockets (CAPS): Short

1. Price establishes a swing low point where the 14-period ADX is above 20. This just means there is at least a moderately strong trend in place.

2. Instead of calculating Fibonacci price resistance levels, wait for a swing high to be completed. Now, let's calculate Fibonacci price support levels using retracements, extensions, projections, and expansions.

3. There are over 1.7 points of "Air Pocket" between FibZone #1 and FibZone #2, which should provide a short opportunity if FibZone #1 is violated to the downside.

4. As price trades back down from point (2), the ADX drops below 20. Price moves down and through FibZone #1 and a possible short entry is made just below 46.35.

5. A stop is placed around $49, which is the previous bar's high.

6. This strategy is more powerful when there has been a previous test of FibZone #1, as seen above. By testing the zone prior to violating, it gives more reason for sell off upon violation. Same day profit of 1.7 points.

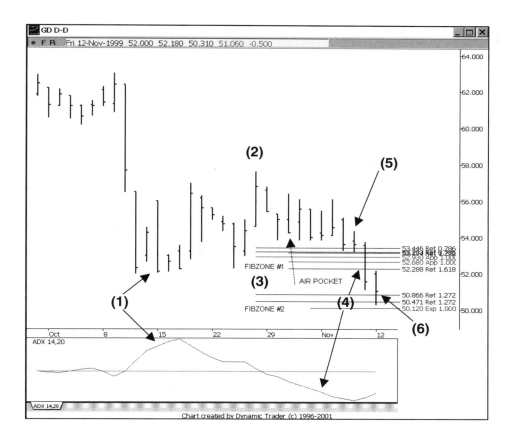

Chart created by Dynamic Trader (c) 1996-2001

## Continuation Air Pockets (CAPS): Short

1. Price establishes a swing low point where the 14-period ADX is above 20. This just means there is at least a moderately strong trend in place.

2. Instead of calculating Fibonacci price resistance levels, wait for a swing high to be completed. Now, let's calculate Fibonacci price support levels using retracements, extensions, projections, and expansions.

3. There are over 1.4 points of "Air Pocket" between FibZone #1 and FibZone #2, which should provide a short opportunity if FibZone #1 is violated to the downside.

4. As price trades back down from point (2), the ADX drops below 20. Price moves down and through FibZone #1 and a possible short entry is made just below 52.28.

5. A stop is placed just above $54, which is the previous bar's high.

6. Two days later the potential to take 1.7 points of profits off the table is available.

## STRATEGY Q&A

*Question: Why use the ADX with these Air Pockets?*

*Answer:* First of all, its good to understand the different readings of the ADX. I have learned to look at the ADX this way:

| | |
|---|---|
| 0–15 | Non-trending market |
| 16–20 | New trend gaining strength |
| 21–40 | Trend strength in full swing |
| >40 | Extreme levels of strength likely to reverse down soon |

So, I chose to use 20 as my focus ADX number. An Air Pocket mixed with a reading that has crossed from above 20 to below 20 signifies a reversal that might be in the works. At the least, the chart will be in non-trending mode. So, with this understanding of the ADX and price violating a FibZone at the same time creates nice Reversal Air Pockets (RAPS). Now, to completely focus on reversal trading is probably a loser's game. You need an arsenal of tools that will help you find trend continuation trades. The Continuation Air Pockets (CAPS) are perfect for this. As an ADX establishes itself above the 20 level then falls slightly below it, it is creating a little "trap," in my opinion. See, the trend may be taking its time and resting for a while along the way. That puts traders to sleep. So, when you have a trend in place and a little ADX trap (above/below 20 shake out) then price action resumes its trend, it can create powerful trading opportunities. Bottom line: ADX is a great filter for Air Pocket setups.

*Question: Do any price levels have to be deleted to create an Air Pocket?*

*Answer:* Yes. If you remember a FibZone is only valid if there are three price levels coming together in a relatively tight range. So, if there are two FibZones nicely defined and between those two FibZones sits one Fibonacci price level all by itself, I will delete that price level and a clear Air Pocket will be identified. Even if two price levels are floating between FibZones I will delete them. Why? Because we need three. Three is the magic number for a FibZone.

*Question: What time frame(s) work best with this strategy?*

*Answer:* The lowest I will go is a 60-minute chart and the highest is a weekly chart. My sweet spot is the daily time frame. It creates Air Pockets anywhere between 1 and 10 points, while anything below 60 typically creates pennies of Air Pocket opportunity.

*Question: You mention that there are three places to consider placing stops; (in the case of a long setup) below the current bar low (the bar triggered into the long trade), below the previous bar low, or below FibZone #1. How do I know which one to use?*

*Answer:* Stop placement involves thinking through a couple of things. First, identifying how much of the Air Pocket profit potential is between FibZone #1 and FibZone #2. Second, knowing how much you can risk in a trade. So, in a situation where the Air Pocket only presents the potential for 1 point of profit, by placing my stop below the previous bar low I will expose myself to 3 points of risk. Consistently putting myself in trades like this is a loser's game. So, the placement of the stop must be changed and brought in tighter to perhaps the current day's low. The other way to deal with this situation is to adjust the number of shares you are trading to account for the higher point risk in the trade. Knowing how many shares to trade is a function of knowing how much capital in your trading account can be at risk on each trade. That "per trade risk amount" is then divided by the number of points of risk in the trade you are considering. The result is the number of shares to trade with in the trade setup you are looking at.

*Question: Do you ever continue to hold these positions beyond the objective of FibZone #2?*

*Answer:* Depending upon position size, I have at times taken half of my position off at FibZone #2 and moved my stop to breakeven on the rest. This definitely keeps you in the game in the situation that price continues to move in your direction. I also think this kind of money management works best when trading CAPS, because you are trading WITH the current trend.

# SECTION III

# IT BOILS DOWN TO PROPER EXECUTION

CHAPTER **11**

# ENTRY PATTERNS: HOW TO ENTER THE TRADE

$\mathbf{A}$ temptation that many Fibonacci traders succumb to is to enter a trade when a Fibonacci strategy merely indicates the possibility of a tradable move. *That is **not** proper execution.* To trade Fibonacci successfully and gain consistent results, you must make sure that you observe price action that confirms that a tradable move is occurring. *Then and only then, can you enter a trade.* In this chapter, the topic of entering trades will be our main focus and I will teach you the best entry methods that I have found.

The best approach that I have found for entering trades is to do the following after you have identified a trading setup:

**Find a trigger pattern in a lower time frame.**

For example, if a setup is occurring on a daily chart, I will drill down to a 60-minute or 30-minute chart to look for triggers.

## What Chart Time Frame Should I Be Looking For a Trigger?

| Setup Occurs | Look for triggers on |
|---|---|
| Weekly | Daily and 60-minute chart |
| Daily | 60- and 30-minute chart |
| 30 | 13- and 8-minute chart |
| 13 | 5-minute chart |

## Trigger Patterns That I Use

Now that we've established the time frames to look at to be triggered into trades, let's look at the types of triggers I use.

Trigger list:

    **1.** Candlesticks

        Doji
        Morning Doji Star
        Evening Doji Star
        Morning Star
        Evening Star
        Shooting Star
        Bearish 3 Method
        Bullish 3 Method
        Hanging Man

Tweezer Bottoms
Tweezer Tops
Bearish Engulfing
Bullish Engulfing

In addition to Candlesticks, I also use more complex patterns on lower time frames after identifying a potential trade on a higher time frame. Some of these patterns will sound familiar because they are trading strategies that I taught you in earlier chapters. However, they are highly useful as entry triggers in lower time frames. I will give you clear illustrations of this concept later in this chapter.

**2.** Two-Step Patterns

Symmetrical TSP
Gartley TSP
Butterfly TSP

**3.** Old School Patterns:

Double Top
Double Bottom
Head & Shoulders
Reverse Head & Shoulders

# MY FAVORITE CANDLESTICK ENTRY PATTERNS

## Introduction

Japanese rice traders developed candlesticks centuries ago to visually display price activity over a defined trading period. Each candlestick represents the trading activity for one period. The lines of a candlestick represent the open, high, low and close for that particular period.

The main body (the wide part) of the candlestick represents the range between the opening and closing price. If the closing price is greater than the opening price, the main body is white. If the closing price is less than the opening price the main body is black. The lines coming out of each end represent the highest high and lowest low of that particular period and are commonly referred to as wicks, shadows, or tails.

One can use candlestick patterns as a trigger to enter a trade on the same time frame the setup occurs, or drill down to the appropriate time frame mentioned on the previous page, based on the time frame of the setup.

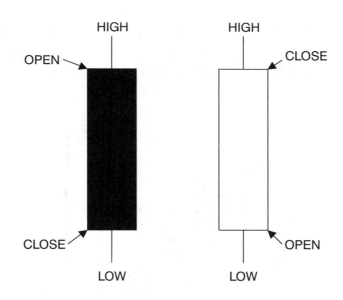

Now, let's run through the basic candlestick patterns I look for to trigger me into a trade.

## Entry Patterns

Below are graphic representations of each candlestick pattern I look for:

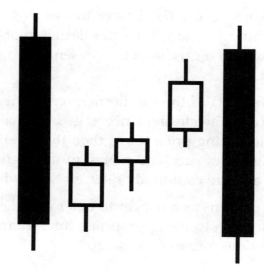

**Bearish 3 Method:** A long black body followed by a few small bodies and ending in another long black body. The small bodies are usually contained within the first black body's range. This is a bearish continuation pattern.

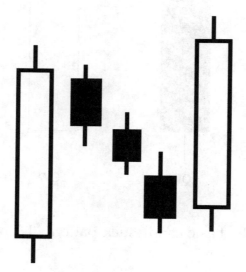

**Bullish 3 Method:** A long white body followed by a few small bodies and ending in another long white body. The small bodies are usually contained within the first white body's range. This is a bullish continuation pattern.

**Doji:** The open and close are the same so no "body" exists on this candle. This candle assumes longer-term significance the longer the vertical lines above and/or below the open and close horizontal line. Typically the doji represents indecision between buyers and sellers and a high likelihood for reversal exists after this candlestick is complete.

**Bearish Engulfing:** A small white body followed by and contained within a larger dark body candlestick. This is a top reversal pattern and typically leads to an initiation of a sell off.

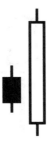

**Bullish Engulfing:** A small dark body followed by and contained within a larger white body candlestick. This is a bottom reversal pattern and typically leads to an initiation of a rally.

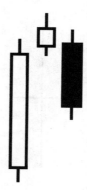

**Evening Star:** a large white body followed by a small body that gaps above the white body. The third candlestick is a black body that closes 50% or more into the white body. This is a top reversing pattern

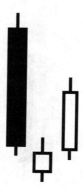

**Morning Star:** a large dark body followed by a small body that gaps below the dark body. The third candlestick is a white body that closes 50% or more into the dark body. This is a bottom reversing pattern.

**Hanging Man:** Small body near the high with a long lower tail with little or no upper tail. This is a bearish pattern during an uptrend.

**Shooting Star:** A candlestick with a small body at or around the low with a long upper tail and little or no lower tail. This is a bearish pattern in an uptrend.

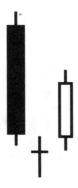

**Morning Doji Star:** A large dark body followed by a doji that gaps down below the black candle. The next candlestick is a white candle that closes at least 50% into the dark candle. This is a bottom reversing pattern.

**Evening Doji Star:** A large white body followed by a doji that gaps up above the white candle. The next candlestick is a dark candle that closes at least 50% into the white candle. This is a top reversing pattern.

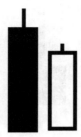

**Tweezer Bottom:** Two candlesticks with matching bottoms. Ideally, the first candle is a dark candle and the close is at the low, and the second candle is a white candle with the open at the low. This typically represents a short-term low at the least.

**Tweezer Top:** These are two or more candles with similar tops. Ideally, the first candle is a white candle and the close is at or near the high. The second candlestick opens at the high and typically has a higher tail and either a dark or white body below it. This typically represents a short-term top, at the least.

The candlestick patterns I've shown you speak volumes about market sentiment and shifts in supply and demand of a particular stock, commodity, or futures contract. I believe candlestick-pattern recognition and Fibonacci price analysis is unrivaled in their combined accuracy to define high-probability trading opportunities. There are countless software programs available that can scan for candlestick patterns of the entire universe of publicly traded securities in seconds, and kick out results of all the charts that possess any one of the candlestick patterns I've mentioned in this chapter. My favorite book on this subject is *Candlestick Charting Explained* by Gregory Morris, if you would like further information on this subject.

Now, let me put these triggers together with trading setups and show you how they are used. The best way to apply the trigger patterns I've shown you involves identifying a setup on a certain time frame, and then drilling down to a lower time frame to look for either a candlestick entry pattern by itself or one of the following more complex patterns.

> Double Tops & Bottoms
> Head & Shoulders/Reverse Head & Shoulders
> Gartley TSP
> Butterfly TSP
> Symmetrical TSP
> Shark Attack

## A couple of warnings here:

1.  If you are looking at a weekly chart setup, remember to only drill down one or two time frames below the weekly chart to look for triggers. Otherwise, if you start trying to look for triggers on a 5-minute chart for that weekly chart setup, you will likely get whipsawed out of your position quite often. So use the timetable guide mentioned earlier as a reference when looking for triggers.

2.  Always be aware of at least one time frame higher than your setup. Higher time frames ALWAYS carry more significance and weight on price movement. So, if you have a bearish setup on a 30-minute chart and you are looking for triggers to go short on, say, a 13-minute chart, stop looking for triggers until you have confirmed the larger picture is not setting up in the opposite direction. *Always, always, always be aware of the higher time frame.*

## Examples of Triggers on Lower Time Frames

Below we have a daily chart of EBAY. The stock had been in the midst of a significant sell off for a few weeks as it was approaching one of our Support FibZones. It was also completing a Bullish Butterfly TSP into this FibZone. So, when a stock is moving like a freight train to the downside, we want some kind of confirmation of a reversal to the upside. So, I pull out the microscope and drill down into price activity on lower time frames around the area of pattern completion and around our FibZone.

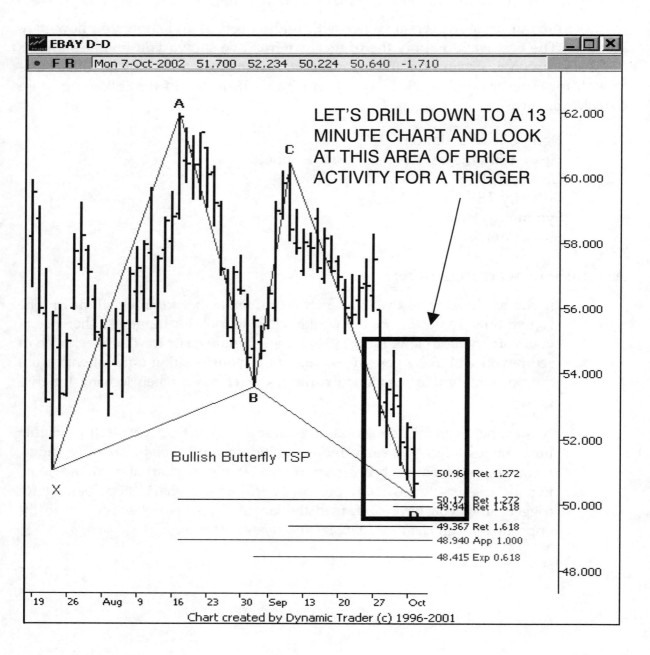

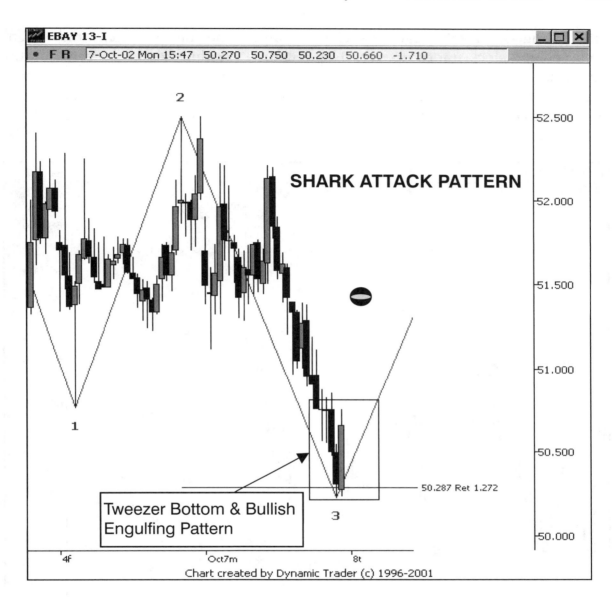

There are two triggers on this 13-minute chart of EBAY.

   **A.** A Shark Attack Pattern labeled 1, 2, 3. Remember this is where price extends to 1.272 or 1.618 of swing 1:2.

   **B.** In fact, at the 1.272 extension of this pattern on the 13-minute chart, EBAY puts in a Tweezer Bottom and Bullish Engulfing Candlestick Pattern. The combination of these two triggers gives me the confidence to take a long trade.

The completion of one or both of these patterns would serve as a legitimate trigger to take the long trade in EBAY.

After seeing two great triggers develop on lower time frames, a long trade is entered and the stock trades up over 14 points in 13 trading sessions. Partial profits would have been taken between the .50 and .618 retracement of Swing C:D. Once those profits were booked, I would trail my stop up to at least breakeven. Then my final objective on the trade is up at the 1.272 to 1.618 extension of swing C:D.

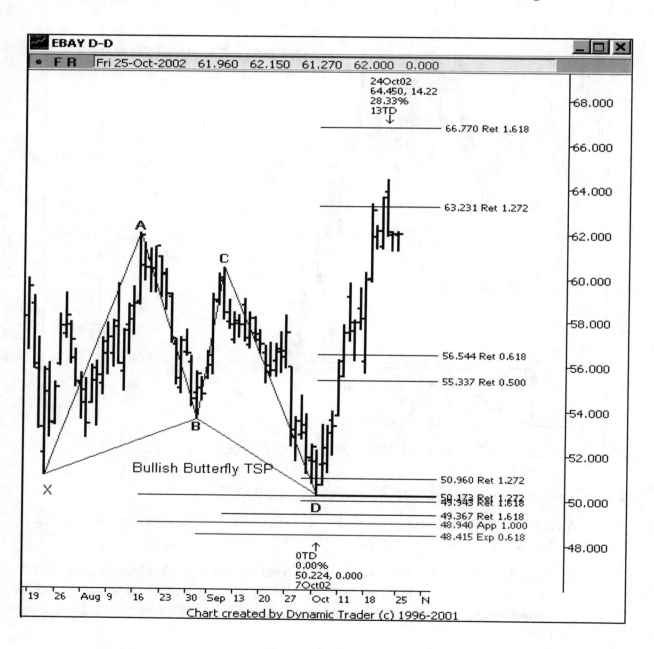

Below we have a 30-minute chart of AFFX. It was in the midst of a decent-size rally. However, it was also completing a Shark Attack Pattern on this time frame into a Resistance FibZone. With a trend to the upside in place, and a bearish reversal pattern unfolding, I wanted to wait for a trigger on a lower time frame to take me into a short trade. So, once again, I pull out the microscope and drill down into price activity on lower time frames around the area of pattern completion and around our FibZone.

AFFX 30-I

● **F R**   6-Nov-02 Wed 14:30   27.630   27.830   27.561   27.830   1.050

27.893 App 0.618

27.752 Ret 1.618

27.524 Ret 1.618
27.482 Ret 1.272

LET'S DRILL DOWN TO A 13 MINUTE CHART AND LOOK AT THIS AREA OF PRICE ACTIVITY FOR A TRIGGER.

Chart created by Dynamic Trader (c) 1996-2001

Once AFFX went up into our FibZone, I pulled up a 13-minute chart and started looking for reasons to take a short trade. There was a combination of four candlesticks on this time frame that caused me to pull the trigger. See below.

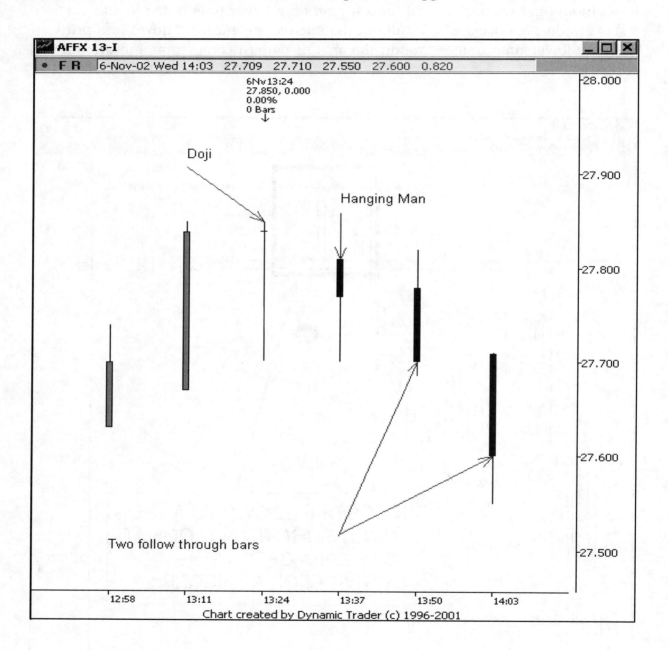

After the candlesticks triggered us in, AFFX does not make a new high and it trades down over 6% the next day, or 1.75 points.

# TO REVIEW

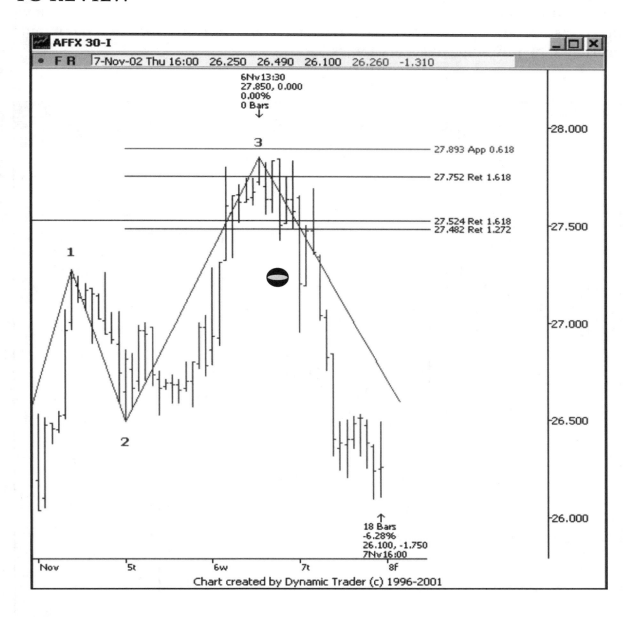

- We found a possible pattern setup on a 30-minute chart.

- Drill down one or two time frames lower for a trigger. A trigger can be any of the candlesticks or other patterns we mentioned in this book.

- Once the trigger/pattern completes on the lower time frame, enter the trade.

On June 19, 2002, LPNT is completing a Bearish Gartley TSP Pattern. If you are not interested in taking the simple trigger, which is entering on a trade below the previous bar's low after pattern completion, we were able to drill down to a 60- minute chart and identify some reversal candlestick patterns.

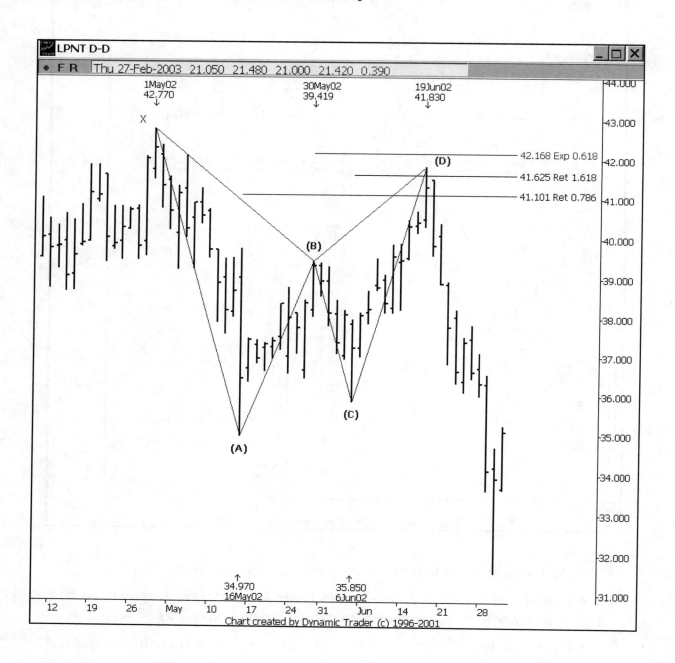

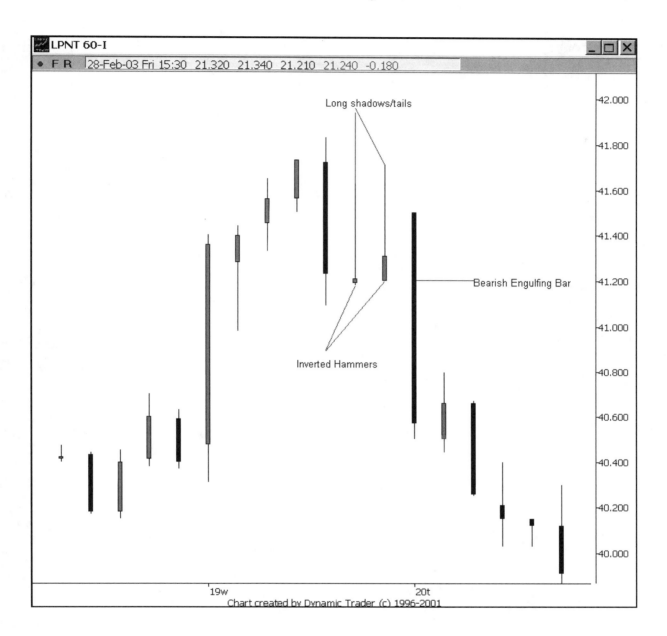

The candlesticks that showed up against our Resistance FibZone off the daily chart and the Bearish Gartley TSP gave me confidence to take the short sometime between 40 and 41. As you saw from the previous chart, LPNT ended up trading almost 10 points lower in the coming sessions.

CHAPTER **12**

# RISK MANAGEMENT: IDENTIFYING AND MANAGING THE KEY AREAS OF RISK CONTROL

Now that I have taught you my best Fibonacci trading strategies, I want to do everything I can to help you get the most benefit from them.

For each of the trading strategies I have taught you in this book, I have provided you with trade management techniques to keep potential losses under control. But strategy and money management are only two ingredients that are necessary for long-term success in trading the financial markets.

No matter how well you understand the step-by-step process of applying these strategies and managing the trades, this knowledge will only benefit you if you have the discipline to execute the strategies properly. That is what most people have the greatest degree of difficulty with.

## WHY IS PROPER EXECUTION SO DIFFICULT?

I have seen many people come into this business who have been successful in other walks of life, like doctors, engineers, attorneys, etc. The success these people have achieved in their previous careers was largely attributed to their ability to perfect their skills. Unfortunately, they quickly discover that there is no method of trading that allows you to become 100% accurate or "perfect." This simple fact drives people out of this business.

When someone has a string of two or three losses, they feel defeated and either blame the losses on themselves or redirect that feeling of failure to the system being used. Once this happens, they start to second-guess their strategy or change the rules. Soon their losses pile up and the pain becomes so intolerable that they give up.

I maintain that the weakness that people have is that they direct their innate desire for perfection to the wrong aspects of trading.

- The common tendency is to focus on perfect performance in the form of a high percentage of winning to losing trades.

Fortunately, I believe there is a way to *turn that weakness into a strength*. To become a successful trader, you can still aim for perfection. Here's how:

- Rather than focusing on perfect outcomes for every trade, you must instead focus on **perfect execution of every trade.**

That is, when you have a viable trading method, you must be completely committed to executing its prescribed steps together with trade management, perfectly. Only by repeating this process over and over again and never deviating from it, do you have a solid foundation for success.

*This is not easy to do, at least initially.*

The reason is that the process of trading tends to stir up deep emotions that seriously wreak havoc to one's decision-making ability. This where **psychology** comes into play.

In order to trade successfully, you must have a framework for executing each of the rules of your trading strategy that does not allow your emotions to impact the process. Controlling your emotions is a broad topic that I am not an expert on. But I know from first-hand experience that it is critical to executing each trade properly.

In terms of learning how to control your emotions while trading, I'll leave that to the experts.

I recommend you read *Trading In The Zone* by Mark Douglas. It is a requirement for anyone that I mentor in trading. The other book that I have found extremely valuable in this area is *The Tao Of Trading* by Robert Koppel.

Now, we have covered strategy, execution, money management and psychology. Restating these factors in a different way, the formula for success in trading is:

**Strategy + Execution + Money Management + Proper Psychology =
Trading Success**

I could write an entire book on the topic of this formula. But since that is not the main purpose of this book, I will instead give you the knowledge that I consider to be the starting point for trading success.

## CONTROLLING RISK EXPOSURE

If you want to become a successful trader, the best starting point is to master your ability to control risk. With every strategy that I have taught you in this book, I have included money management rules. All of the examples I took you through, employ the use of stops and trailing stops. But managing individual trades is only one aspect of risk control. I have found that there are many other risk variables, and the more awareness and control that you have over them, the better your trading performance will be.

I have built a checklist to walk through every night as I prepare for the next trading day.

1.  **Directional Exposure:**

    How many long trades and how many short trades do you have in play right now? Are you overweighted in a certain direction based on the current position of the overall market?

2.  **Sector Exposure:**

    Of the positions you have, is there any one sector in which you are overweighted? If you have three trades in your account and they are all long semiconductor stocks, you are not doing a good job of controlling risk.

3.  **Position Size:**

    Are you only risking a maximum of 2% to 3% of your equity in one trade? Be sure to think and plan this one through very carefully. 2% to 3% works for my account size. However, a different level of risk per trade may be more appropriate for you.

4.  **News Exposure:**

    Are you avoiding being exposed to news (such as earnings announcements) that may have negative or unpredictable effects on any trade that you are in?

5.  **Pattern Exposure:**

    Are you overexposed to one particular trading pattern? Let me explain this further. What happens a few times a year is that the entire market forms the same pattern. You look at the indices and, for example, they are forming a Bullish Gartley TSP pattern on a daily chart. Well, as I do my nightly homework, I find 30 stocks with Bullish Gartleys. How many do I take? My answer to this is one. In situations like this where the entire market is setting up with the same pattern, I trade a market proxy like the ETFs or index futures. Inexperienced traders would see these patterns as tons of opportunity and lots of profit potential, and consistently lose. The trader who consistently wins sees this as a major risk. The winning trader thinks, "What if this pattern fails and I'm long all these daily Bullish Gartley patterns?" The pattern can be a high percentage trade, but if the market breaks down and the pattern fails on the index level, guess what? It is highly likely that all 30 of those other patterns fail as well. In reality that is only one failed pattern. Bottom line: Be smart in allocating among various types of patterns.

**6. Time Frame Exposure:**

I get asked this question often as well, "What time frame do you trade in?" Well, the answer to that is monthly, weekly, daily, 60-minute, and 30-minute charts. Personally, I think it is extremely unhealthy to have all trades based on one time frame. Mix it up, and have longer term trades and shorter-term trades in the account. This is a great diversifier and personally it keeps me sharp and aware of what the markets are looking like on these different time frames. Analyzing multiple time frames of a security is like watching a story unfold or even watching a well-choreographed dance. These different time frames are interrelated and have an action/reaction relationship.

**7. Total Portfolio Risk:**

This is straight forward. If all your positions were stopped out today, how much of a hit would it be to your account? If your answer is more than 20%–25%, I would caution you to rethink the total portfolio risk exposure. Bad things happen to extremely talented traders. This is something you can control!

Do not get me wrong here. The goal of trading is to attain high absolute positive returns annually (at least that's my goal). To do this and attack it with intensity, you must first identify and manage risk. Once it is identified and boundaries are in place, be aggressive, take charge and expect to succeed.

I will leave you with a few of my favorite "mental" quotes as they have significant meaning to our business of trading as well as life:

1. "Your mind is a sacred enclosure into which nothing harmful can enter except by your permission." – Ralph Waldo Emerson

2. "The less I think, the better I will do." – David Lansburgh

3. ". . . Being in control of the mind means that literally anything that happens can be a source of joy . . ." – Mihaly Csikszentmihalyi

4. " . . . exercise unrelenting discipline over your thought patterns. Cultivate only productive attitudes . . . You are the product of everything you put into your body and mind." – I Ching

5. "The greatest efforts . . . come when the mind is as still as a glass lake." – Timothy Gallway

6. "Let the market, not your ego, make the decisions." – Ed Toppel

7. "Positive emotional state leads to optimum trading performance." – Robert Koppel

8. And here are my favorite quotes from Mark Douglas:

   - "Trying to avoid something that is unavoidable will have disastrous effects on your ability to trade successfully."

   - "The best traders aren't afraid."

   - "Ninety-Five percent of the trading errors . . . stem from your attitudes about being wrong, losing money, missing out, and leaving money on the table."

   - ". . . there are no limits to the market's behavior."

   - "Market analysis is not the path to consistent results."

   - "Even though the outcome of each individual pattern is random, the outcome of a series of patterns is consistent (statistically reliable). This is a paradox, but one that is easily resolved with a disciplined, organized, and consistent approach."

   - "Attitude produces better overall results than analysis or technique."

   - "Losing and being wrong are inevitable realities of trading."

   - "It does not do you any good to take the risk of putting on a trade if you are afraid of the consequences, because your fears will act on your perception of information and your behavior in a way that will cause you to create the very experience you fear the most, the one you are trying to avoid."

   - "Each trade is simply an edge with a probable outcome, and statistically independent of every other trade. If you believe otherwise, then I can see why you're afraid; but I can assure you that your fears are completely unfounded."

   - "One of your basic objectives as a trader is to perceive the opportunities available, not the threat of pain."

   - "If you asked me to distill trading down to its simplest form, I would say that it is a pattern recognition numbers game. We use market analysis to identify the patterns, define risk, and determine when to take profits. The trade either works or it doesn't. In any case, we move on to the next trade. It's that simple, but it's certainly not easy. In fact, trading is probably the hardest thing you'll ever attempt to be successful at."

## CLOSING THOUGHTS

I hope you have enjoyed reading and learning about the many facets of trading with Fibonacci. It was my goal to give you an in-depth exposure to Fibonacci time and price analysis and to enable you to calculate Support and Resistance FibZones. With that base knowledge of creating FibZones, it was my goal to equip you with high-probability strategies using these FibZones. Finally, I wanted to stress the part of trading that doesn't involve strategy. So much of trading success has nothing to do with strategy and all to do with money management and mental approach. Finally, I believe a trader can walk away with one or two of these strategies and when incorporated into "The Formula" for success, will achieve solid results.

I have officially passed on to you an "edge" in the market place. Now it's up to you to decide what to do with it.

**Derrik Hobbs**

# BIBLIOGRAPHY

Bigalow, Steve. *Profitable Candlestick Trading*. New York: John Wiley & Sons, 2002.

Carney, Scott M. *The Harmonic Trader*. Scott M. Carney, 1999.

DiNapoli, Joe. *Trading with DiNapoli Levels*. Sarasota, F.L.: Coast Investment Software, 1998.

Douglas, Mark. *The Disciplined Trader: Developing Winning Attitudes*. Paramus, N.J.: New York Institute of Finance, 1990.

Douglas, Mark. *Trading In The Zone*. Paramus, N.J.: New York Institute of Finance, 2000.

Elder, Alexander. *Trading for a Living*. New York: John Wiley & Sons, 1993.

Farley, Alan S. *The Master Swing Trader*. New York: McGraw Hill, 2001.

Fischer, Robert. *The New Fibonacci Trader*. New York: John Wiley & Sons, 2001.

Gartley, H. M. *Profits in the Stock Market*. Pomeroy, W.A.: Lambert-Gann, 1935.

Gilmore, Bryce T. *Geometry of Markets*. Australia: Bryce Gilmore & Associates, Pty. Ltd, 1989.

———. *Geometry of Markets, II*, Australia: Bryce Gilmore & Associates, Pty. Ltd, 1993.

Koppel, Robert. *The Tao of Trading*, Chicago: Dearborn Financial Publishing, 2001.

Landry, Dave. *Dave Landry on Swing Trading*. Los Angeles, C.A.: M. Gordon Publishing, Inc., 2001.

Miner, Robert C. *Dynamic Trading*. Tucson, A.Z.: Dynamic Traders Group, Inc., 1999.

Morris, Gregory. *Candlestick Charting Explained*. New York: McGraw-Hill, 1995.

Murphy, John J. *Technical Analysis of the Financial Markets*. New York: McGraw-Hill, 1995.

Nison, Steve. *Japanese Candlestick Charting*. Paramus, N.J.: New York Institute of Finance, 1991.

Pesavento, Larry. *Fibonacci Ratios with Pattern Recognition*. South Carolina: Traders Press, Inc., 1997.

Prechter, Robert. *Elliott Wave Principle*. Georgia: New Classics Library, 1978.

Pring, Martin. *Martin Pring on Market Momentum*. New York: McGraw Hill, 1993.

Von Oech, Roger. *Expect The Unexpected Or You Won't Find It*. San Francisco, C.A.: Berrett-Koehler Publishers, 2002.

Wilder, J. Welles. *New Concepts in Technical Trading Systems*, North Carolina: Trend Research, 1978.

# ABOUT THE AUTHOR

Derrik Hobbs is a money manager for a publicly traded mutual fund. The Fund was listed as one of the best performing funds in their universe in the January 2002 issue of *Smart Money*. Derrik provides short- to intermediate-term trading guidance to the Fund, as well as entry and exit recommendations on long-term fundamental positions, based on technical indicators and Fibonacci analysis. Derrik is also the manager of a hedge fund that incorporates the Fibonacci strategies outlined in this book.